THE

C

ANSWER BOOK

THE

C

ANSWER BOOK

Solutions to the Exercises in
The C Programming Language
by Brian W. Kernighan & Dennis M. Ritchie

Clovis L. Tondo

Scott E. Gimpel

PRENTICE-HALL, INC., Englewood Cliffs, New Jersey 07632

This book was set in English Times and Typewriter
Elite by UNICOMP of Los Alamos, NM using a Compu-
graphic 8400 typesetter driven by a PDP-11/73 running the UNIX operating system.

UNIX is a Trademark of AT&T Bell Laboratories.

Library of Congress Catalog Card Number: 85-60474

ISBN: 0-13-109877-2

Printed in the United States of America

10   9   8   7

ISBN 0-13-109877-2   01

Prentice-Hall International (UK) Limited, *London*
Prentice-Hall of Australia Pty. Limited, *Sydney*
Prentice-Hall Canada Inc., *Toronto*
Prentice-Hall Hispanoamericana, S.A., *Mexico*
Prentice-Hall of India Private Limited, *New Delhi*
Prentice-Hall of Japan, Inc., *Tokyo*
Prentice-Hall of Southeast Asia Pte. Ltd., *Singapore*
Editora Prentice-Hall do Brasil, Ltda., *Rio de Janeiro*
Whitehall Books Limited, *Wellington, New Zealand*

CONTENTS

PREFACE

This is an ANSWER BOOK. It provides solutions to all the exercises in *The C Programming Language* by Brian W. Kernighan and Dennis M. Ritchie (Prentice-Hall, 1978)*. Careful study of *The C Answer Book*, used in conjunction with K&R, will help you understand C and teach you good C programming skills.

Use K&R to learn C, work the exercises, then study the solutions presented here. We built our solutions using the language constructs known at the time the exercises appear in K&R. The intent is to follow the pace of K&R. Later, when you learn more language constructs, you will be able to provide possibly better solutions. For example, until the construct

```
if (expression)
        statement-1
else
        statement-2
```

is explained on page 19 K&R, we do not use it. However, you could improve the solutions to Exercises 1-6, 1-7, and 1-8 (page 18 K&R) by using it. At times we also present unconstrained solutions.

On page 14 K&R there is a description of symbolic constants. When a solution uses standard symbolic constants, such as EOF, you notice the line

```
#include <stdio.h>
```

The header file stdio.h contains macros and symbolic constants used by the standard I/O library. Refer to pages 143 K&R and 165 K&R for detailed information on stdio.h.

---

* Hereafter referred to as K&R.

We explain the solutions. We presume you have read the material in K&R up to the exercise. We try not to repeat K&R, but describe the highlights of each solution.

You cannot learn a programming language by only reading the language constructs. It also requires programming — writing your own code and studying those of others. We use good features of the language, modularize our code, make extensive use of library routines, and format our programs to help the reader see the logical flow.

We owe our debt to the pioneers in the C Language, Brian W. Kernighan and Dennis M. Ritchie, whose genius and style we model our work after. We further thank Brian W. Kernighan for his thorough reviews of our work. We also thank our editor Karl V. Karlstrom.

We are grateful to our friend Ramsey W. Haddad of Stanford University. He picked at our manuscript far beyond our expectations and discovered problems we overlooked. His friendship, support, and influence will always be greatly appreciated.

This book was typeset by Walt Brainerd of UNICOMP, Los Alamos, NM. The job performed was far beyond our expectations; we acknowledge his professionalism and meticulous work.

Our thanks also to Phillip M. Adams, Patricia A. Gates, Stephen L. Mackey, and our parents, who helped us in one form or another along the way.

Clovis L. Tondo

Scott E. Gimpel

THE

C

ANSWER BOOK

CHAPTER 1: **A TUTORIAL INTRODUCTION**

Exercise 1-1:   (page 6 K&R)

Run this program on your system. Experiment with leaving out parts of the program, to see what error messages you get.

```
main()
{
    printf("hello, world");
}
```

In this example, the newline (\n) character is missing. This causes the output not to be followed by a line feed (new line).

```
main()
{
    printf("hello, world\n")
}
```

In the second example, the semicolon is missing after printf(). Every C statement must be terminated by a semicolon (page 9 K&R). The compiler should recognize this as an error, and print the appropriate message.

```
main()
{
    printf("hello, world\n');
}
```

In the third example, the double quote " after \n is missing. The single quote along with the right parenthesis and semicolon is taken as part of the string. The compiler should recognize this as an error, and either complain that a double quote is missing or that the string is too long.

Exercise 1-2: (page 7 K&R)

Experiment to find out what happens when printf's argument string contains \x, where x is some character not listed above.

```
main()
{
    printf("hello, world\a");
    printf("hello, world\7");
    printf("hello, world\?");
}
```

The C Reference Manual (Appendix A, page 181 K&R) states,

> if the character following a backslash is not one of those specified, the backslash is ignored.

In the June 1983 version of The C Programming Language - Reference Manual by Dennis Ritchie (it is Appendix A from K&R with changes),

> if the character following a backslash is not one of those specified, the behavior is undefined.

The result of this experiment is compiler dependent. One possible result might be

```
hello, worldahello, world<BELL>hello, world?
```

where <BELL> is a short beep produced by ASCII 7.

Exercise 1-3:   (page 11 K&R)

Modify the temperature conversion program to print a heading above
the table.

```
main()    /* Fahrenheit-Celsius table for fahr = 0, 20, ..., 300 */
{
    int lower, upper, step;
    float fahr, celsius;

    lower = 0;                /* lower limit of temperature table */
    upper = 300;              /* upper limit                      */
    step  = 20;               /* step size                        */

    printf("Fahr Celsius\n");
    fahr = lower;
    while (fahr <= upper) {
        celsius = (5.0/9.0) * (fahr-32.0);
        printf("%4.0f %6.1f\n", fahr, celsius);
        fahr = fahr + step;
    }
}
```

The addition of

```
printf("Fahr Celsius\n");
```

before the loop produces a heading above the appropriate columns. The
remainder of the program is the same as on page 8 K&R.

Exercise 1-4:   (page 11 K&R)

Write a program to print the corresponding Celsius to Fahrenheit table.

```
main() /* Celsius-Fahrenheit table for celsius = 0, 20, ..., 300 */
{
    int lower, upper, step;
    float fahr, celsius;

    lower = 0;                /* lower limit of temperature table */
    upper = 300;              /* upper limit                      */
    step = 20;                /* step size                        */

    printf("Celsius  Fahr\n");
    celsius = lower;
    while (celsius <= upper) {
        fahr = (9.0*celsius) / 5.0 + 32.0;
        printf("%4.0f %6.1f\n", celsius, fahr);
        celsius = celsius + step;
    }
}
```

A table is produced containing temperatures in degrees Celsius (0 - 300) and their equivalent Fahrenheit values. Fahrenheit is calculated using the known value of Celsius through the statement:

```
fahr = (9.0*celsius) / 5.0 + 32.0;
```

The solution follows the same logic as used in the program that prints the Fahrenheit-Celsius table (page 8 K&R). The integer variables lower, upper, and step refer to the lower limit, upper limit, and step size of the variable celsius, respectively. The variable celsius is initialized to the lower limit, and inside the while loop the equivalent Fahrenheit temperature is calculated. The Celsius and equivalent Fahrenheit values are printed, and the variable celsius is incremented by the step size. The while loop repeats until the variable celsius exceeds its upper limit.

Exercise 1-5:   (page 12 K&R)

Modify the temperature conversion program to print the table in reverse order, that is, from 300 degrees to 0.

```
main() /* Fahrenheit-Celsius table for fahr = 300, 280, ..., 0 */
{
    int fahr;

    for (fahr = 300; fahr >= 0; fahr = fahr - 20)
        printf("%4d %6.1f\n", fahr, (5.0/9.0)*(fahr-32));
}
```

The only modification is:

```
for (fahr = 300; fahr >= 0; fahr = fahr - 20)
```

The first part of the for statement,

```
fahr = 300
```

initializes the Fahrenheit variable (fahr) to its upper limit. The second part, or the condition that controls the for loop,

```
fahr >= 0
```

tests whether the Fahrenheit variable exceeds or meets its lower limit. The for loop continues as long as the statement is true. The reinitialization step,

```
fahr = fahr - 20
```

decrements the Fahrenheit variable by its step size.

Exercise 1-6: (page 18 K&R)

Write a program to count blanks, tabs, and newlines.

```
#include <stdio.h>

main()                        /* count blanks, tabs, and newlines */
{
    int c, nb, nt, nl;

    nb = 0;                             /* number of blanks   */
    nt = 0;                             /* number of tabs     */
    nl = 0;                             /* number of newlines */
    while ((c = getchar()) != EOF) {
        if (c == ' ')
            ++nb;
        if (c == '\t')
            ++nt;
        if (c == '\n')
            ++nl;
    }
    printf("%d %d %d\n", nb, nt, nl);
}
```

The integer variables nb, nt, and nl are used to count the number of blanks, tabs, and newlines, respectively. Initially, these three automatic variables are set equal to 0.

Inside the body of the while loop, the occurrence of each blank, tab, and newline fetched from input is recorded. All if statements are executed each time through the loop. If the character fetched is anything but a blank, tab, or newline, then no action is taken. If it is one of these three, then the appropriate counter is incremented. Upon finding an end of file signal (EOF), the results are printed out.

The `if-else` statement is not presented until page 19 K&R. With that knowledge the solution could be:

```
#include  <stdio.h>

main()                          /* count blanks, tabs, and newlines */
{
    int c, nb, nt, nl;

    nb = 0;                                 /* number of blanks   */
    nt = 0;                                 /* number of tabs     */
    nl = 0;                                 /* number of newlines */
    while ((c = getchar()) != EOF) {
        if (c == ' ')
            ++nb;
        else if (c == '\t')
            ++nt;
        else if (c == '\n')
            ++nl;
    }
    printf("%d %d %d\n", nb, nt, nl);
}
```

Exercise 1-7:   (page 18 K&R)

Write a program to copy its input to its output, replacing each string
of one or more blanks by a single blank.

```c
#include   <stdio.h>
#define    NONBLANK   'a'

main()              /* replace string of blanks with a single blank */
{
     int c, lastc;

     lastc = NONBLANK;
     while ((c = getchar()) != EOF) {
          if (c != ' ')
               putchar(c);
          if (c == ' ')
               if (lastc != ' ')
                    putchar(c);
          lastc = c;
     }
}
```

Blanks are searched for and if one is found, a test is made to determine if it
immediately follows another blank. If it does, the blank is ignored, otherwise
it is printed. This ensures that each single blank gets printed and the first
blank of a string of blanks gets printed.

The integer variable c records the ASCII value of the present character
fetched from input, and lastc records the ASCII value of the previous character fetched. The symbolic constant NONBLANK initializes lastc to an arbitrary nonblank character (in this program, 'a' is used).

The first if statement in the body of the while loop handles the occurrence
of nonblanks. These are printed out. The second if statement handles
blanks, and the third if statement tests for a single blank or the first blank
of a string of blanks. Finally, lastc is updated, and the process repeats.

The if-else statement is not presented until page 19 K&R. With that knowledge the solution could be:

```
#include   <stdio.h>
#define    NONBLANK   'a'

main()                /* replace string of blanks with a single blank */
{
     int c, lastc;

     lastc = NONBLANK;
     while ((c = getchar()) != EOF) {
          if (c != ' ')
               putchar(c);
          else if (lastc != ' ')
               putchar(c);
          lastc = c;
     }
}
```

The logical OR (||) operator is also not presented until page 19 K&R. With
that knowledge the solution could be:

```
#include   <stdio.h>
#define    NONBLANK   'a'

main()                /* replace string of blanks with a single blank */
{
     int c, lastc;

     lastc = NONBLANK;
     while ((c = getchar()) != EOF) {
          if (c != ' ' || lastc != ' ')
               putchar(c);
          lastc = c;
     }
}
```

Exercise 1-8:   (page 18 K&R)

Write a program to replace each tab by the three-character sequence
>, *backspace*, -, which prints as ➤, and each backspace by the sim-
ilar sequence ◄. This makes tabs and backspaces visible.

```
#include  <stdio.h>

main()    /* replace tabs and backspaces with a 3 char sequence */
{
    int c;

    while ((c = getchar()) != EOF) {
        if (c == '\t')
            printf("-\b>");
        if (c == '\b')
            printf("-\b<");
        if (c != '\b')
            if (c != '\t')
                putchar(c);
    }
}
```

Three conditions can arise, and are tested for in the body of the while loop.
The character fetched from input can be a tab, a backspace, or anything else.
If a tab or backspace is found, its equivalent three-character sequence is
printed. If neither a tab nor backspace is found, the character is echoed to
output. The while loop is repeated until an end of file signal is found.

On CRT's that can't overstrike, -\b> shows up as > and >\b- shows up as -.
It is better to use -\b> and -\b< because at least the arrowhead will remain.

The if-else statement is not presented until page 19 K&R. With that knowledge the solution could be:

```c
#include  <stdio.h>

main()      /* replace tabs and backspaces with a 3 char sequence */
{
    int c;

    while ((c = getchar()) != EOF) {
        if (c == '\t')
            printf("-\b>");
        else if (c == '\b')
            printf("-\b<");
        else
            putchar(c);
    }
}
```

Exercise 1-9:   (page 19 K&R)

How would you test the word count program? What are some
boundaries?

To test the word count program first try no input. The output should be: 0 0
0 (zero newlines, zero words, zero characters).

Then try a one character word. The output should be: 1 1 2 (one newline,
one word, two characters - a letter followed by a newline character).

Then try a two character word. The output should be: 1 1 3 (one newline,
one word, three characters - two characters followed by a newline character).

In addition, try 2 one character words (the output should be: 1 2 4), and 2
one character words - one word per line (the output should be: 2 2 4).

Some boundaries are:

- no input
- no words - just newlines
- no words - just blanks, tabs, and newlines
- one word per line - no blanks and tabs
- word starting at very beginning
- word starting after some blanks

Exercise 1-10: (page 19 K&R)

Write a program which prints the words in its input, one per line.

```
#include   <stdio.h>
#define    YES        1
#define    NO         0

main()                              /* print words one per line */
{
     int c, inword;

     inword = NO;
     while ((c = getchar()) != EOF) {
         if (c == ' ' || c == '\n' || c == '\t') {
             if (inword == YES) {
                 putchar('\n');          /* finish the word    */
                 inword = NO;
             }
         } else if (inword == NO) {
             inword = YES;               /* beginning of word */
             putchar(c);
         } else                          /* within a word      */
             putchar(c);
     }
}
```

inword is an integer boolean, which records whether the program is currently in a word or not. At the beginning of the program, inword is initialized to NO, since it is not known where a word begins.

The first if statement,

```
if (c == ' ' || c == '\n' || c == '\t')
```

determines whether c is a word separator. If it is, then the second if statement,

```
if (inword == YES)
```

determines whether this word separator signifies an end of a word. If so, a newline is printed and inword is updated; otherwise no action is taken.

If c is not a word separator, then it is either the first character of a word or another character within the word. If it is the beginning of a new word, then inword is updated. In either case, the character is printed.

Exercise 1-11: (page 19 K&R)

Revise the word count program to use a better definition of "word," for example, a sequence of letters, digits and apostrophes that begins with a letter.

```
#include   <stdio.h>
#define    YES      1
#define    NO       0

main()                        /* count lines, words, chars in input */
{                             /* ASCII only                          */
    int c, nl, nw, nc, inword;

    inword = NO;
    nl = nw = nc = 0;
    while ((c = getchar()) != EOF) {
        ++nc;
        if (c == '\n')
            ++nl;
        if (c == ' ' || c == '\n' || c == '\t')
            inword = NO;
        else if (inword == NO) {
            if ((c >= 'a' && c <= 'z') ||   /* lower case?     */
                (c >= 'A' && c <= 'Z')) {   /* or upper case?  */
                inword = YES;
                ++nw;
            }
        } else if ((c >= 'a' && c <= 'z') || /* lower case?     */
                   (c >= 'A' && c <= 'Z') || /* or upper case?  */
                   (c >= '0' && c <= '9') || /* or digit?       */
                   c == '\'' )               /* or apostrophe?  */
            ;                                /* within a word   */
        else
            inword = NO;
    }
    printf("%d %d %d\n", nl, nw, nc);
}
```

The use of the better definition of a word makes it necessary to add three more statements.

```
if ((c >= 'a' && c <= 'z') ||
    (c >= 'A' && c <= 'Z'))
```

determines whether the first character of a word is either an upper case or a lower case letter (ASCII only). If so, it is the start of a new word; inword is updated and the word counter is incremented.

The test

```
else if ((c >= 'a' && c <= 'z') ||
         (c >= 'A' && c <= 'Z') ||
         (c >= '0' && c <= '9') ||
          c == '\'' )
        ;
```

occurs only if the program is currently in a word and a character other than a blank, newline or tab has been found. This test ensures that the word is a sequence of letters, digits, and apostrophes (ASCII only).

The final statement added,

```
else
        inword = NO;
```

is necessary due to additional non-word characters other than blank, newline, and tab. If one of these additional characters is found, then inword is updated in order to reflect being outside of a word.

Exercise 1-12: (page 22 K&R)

Write a program to print a histogram of the lengths of words in its input. It is easiest to draw the histogram horizontally; a vertical orientation is more challenging.

```c
#include  <stdio.h>
#define   MAXHIST   15              /* max length of histogram  */
#define   MAXWORD   11              /* max length of a word     */
#define   YES       1
#define   NO        0

main()                                      /* horizontal histogram */
{
    int c, i, inword, nc;
    int len;                        /* length of each bar       */
    int maxvalue;                   /* maximum value for wl[]    */
    int wl[MAXWORD];                /* word length counters     */

    inword = NO;
    nc = 0;                         /* number of chars in a word */
    for (i = 0; i < MAXWORD; i++)
        wl[i] = 0;
    while ((c = getchar()) != EOF) {
        if (c == ' ' || c == '\n' || c == '\t')  {
            inword = NO;
            if (nc > 0 && nc < MAXWORD)
                ++wl[nc];
            nc = 0;
        } else if (inword == NO) {
            inword = YES;
            nc = 1;                 /* beginning of a new word */
        } else
            ++nc;                   /* within a word            */
    }
    maxvalue = 0;
    for (i = 1; i < MAXWORD; i++)
        if (wl[i] > maxvalue)
            maxvalue = wl[i];                   /* max value found */
```

```
        for (i = 1; i < MAXWORD; i++) {
            printf("%5d - %5d : ", i, wl[i]);
            if (wl[i] > 0) {
                if ((len = (wl[i] * MAXHIST / maxvalue)) <= 0)
                    len = 1;
            } else
                len = 0;
            while (len > 0) {
                putchar('*');
                --len;
            }
            putchar('\n');
        }
}
```

A blank, newline, or tab marks the end of a word. If a word is found (nc > 0) and its length is less than the maximum word length (nc < MAXWORD), then the appropriate word length counter is incremented (++wl[nc]). If no word is found (only blank(s), newline(s), or tab(s)) or the length of the word is out of range (nc >= MAXWORD), then the word length counter is not modified.

When all words have been read in, the maximum value found (maxvalue) is determined from the array wl.

The variable len scales the value in wl[i] according to MAXHIST and maxvalue. When wl[i] is greater than 0, at least one asterisk is printed.

The horizontal histogram is then printed.

```
#include   <stdio.h>
#define    MAXHIST   15          /* max length of histogram   */
#define    MAXWORD   11          /* max length of a word      */
#define    YES        1
#define    NO         0

main()                                   /* vertical histogram */
{
        int c, i, inword, j, nc;
        int maxvalue;                    /* maximum value for wl[]   */
        int wl[MAXWORD];                 /* word length counters     */
```

```
        inword = NO;
        nc = 0;                                  /* number of chars in a word */
        for (i = 0; i < MAXWORD; i++)
            wl[i] = 0;
        while ((c = getchar()) != EOF) {
            if (c == ' ' || c == '\n' || c == '\t')  {
                inword = NO;
                if (nc > 0 && nc < MAXWORD)
                    ++wl[nc];
                nc = 0;
            } else if (inword == NO) {
                inword = YES;
                nc = 1;                          /* beginning of a new word */
            } else
                ++nc;                            /* within a word            */
        }
        maxvalue = 0;
        for (i = 1; i < MAXWORD; i++)
            if (wl[i] > maxvalue)
                maxvalue = wl[i];                        /* max value found */
        for (i = MAXHIST; i > 0; i--) {
            for (j = 1; j < MAXWORD; j++)
                if ((wl[j] * MAXHIST / maxvalue) >= i)
                    printf("  *  ");
                else
                    printf("     ");
            putchar('\n');
        }
        for (i = 1; i < MAXWORD; i++)
            printf("%4d ", i);
        putchar('\n');
        for (i = 1; i < MAXWORD; i++)
            printf("%4d ", wl[i]);
        putchar('\n');
    }
```

This solution prints a vertical histogram. It is similar to the previous program until `maxvalue` is determined. Then, it is necessary to scale each element of the array `wl` and verify if an asterisk should be printed for each one of the elements. This verification is necessary since all bars are printed simultaneously (vertical histogram). The last two `for` loops print the index and value for each element of `wl`.

Exercise 1-13: (page 24 K&R)

Write a program to convert its input to lower case, using a function lower(c) which returns c if c is not a letter, and the lower case value of c if it is a letter.

```
#include   <stdio.h>

main()                              /* convert input to lower case */
{
    int c;

    while ((c = getchar()) != EOF)
        putchar(lower(c));
}

lower(c)
int c;
{
    if (c >= 'A' && c <= 'Z')
        return(c - 'A' + 'a');
    else
        return(c);
}
```

In the function lower, if c is inclusively within the range 'A'-'Z', its lower case equivalent is returned. The expression,

```
c - 'A' + 'a'
```

converts an upper case to its equivalent lower case for the ASCII character set only. If c is anything else, then c is returned.

In the main routine, putchar prints the value returned from lower.

lower is rewritten in Exercise 2-10 using a conditional expression (page 47 K&R).

Exercise 1-14: (page 27 K&R)

Revise the main routine of the longest-line program so it will correctly print the length of arbitrarily long input lines, and as much as possible of the text.

```
#include  <stdio.h>
#define   MAXLINE   1000

main()                              /* find longest line */
{
    int len;                /* current line length      */
    int max;                /* maximum length seen so far */
    char line[MAXLINE];     /* current input line       */
    char save[MAXLINE];     /* longest line, saved      */

    max = 0;
    while ((len = getline(line, MAXLINE)) > 0) {
        printf("%d, %s\n", len, line);
        if (len > max) {
            max = len;
            copy(line, save);
        }
    }
    if (max > 0)                        /* there was a line */
        printf("%s", save);
}
```

```
getline(s, lim)                  /* get line into s, return length */
char s[];
int lim;
{
    int c, i, j;

    j = 0;
    for (i = 0; (c = getchar()) != EOF && c != '\n'; i++)
            if (i < lim-2) {
                    s[j] = c;           /* line still within boundaries */
                    ++j;
            }
    if (c == '\n') {
        s[j] = c;
        ++j;
        ++i;
    }
    s[j] = '\0';
    return(i);
}


copy(s1, s2)                 /* copy s1 to s2; assume s2 big enough */
char s1[], s2[];
{
    int i;

    i = 0;
    while ((s2[i] = s1[i]) != '\0')
            ++i;
}
```

The only revision in the main routine is,

```
printf("%d, %s\n", len, line);
```

This prints the length of the input line (len) and as many characters as it is possible to save in the array line.

The function getline has a few modifications.

```
for (i = 0; (c = getchar()) != EOF && c != '\n'; i++)
```

The test for the number of characters that can be saved in s is no longer performed in the for statement. This limit is not a condition for termination because getline now returns the length of arbitrarily long input lines and saves as much possible of the text. The statement

```
if (i < lim-2)
```

determines if there is room in the array (still within boundaries). The original test in the for loop was

```
i < lim-1
```

It was changed because the last index of the array s is

```
lim-1
```

since s has lim elements. So

```
i < lim-2
```

leaves room for a possible newline character

```
s[lim-2] = '\n';
```

and an end of string marker.

```
s[lim-1] = '\0';
```

The length of the string is returned in i; j keeps track of the number of characters copied to the string s.

Exercise 1-15:   (page 27 K&R)

Write a program to print all lines that are longer than 80 characters.

```
#include   <stdio.h>
#define    LONGLINE   80
#define    MAXLINE    1000              /* maximum input line size */

main()                          /* print lines longer than LONGLINE */
{
     int len;                           /* current line length    */
     char line[MAXLINE];                /* current input line     */

     while ((len = getline(line, MAXLINE)) > 0)
         if (len > LONGLINE)
             printf("%s\n", line);
}
```

A line of text is fetched from input and its length is returned by getline. If the length is greater than 80 characters (LONGLINE), then the input line is printed. Otherwise, no action is taken. This procedure is repeated until all input lines have been fetched.

The function getline is the same as in Exercise 1-14.

Exercise 1-16: (page 27 K&R)

Write a program to remove trailing blanks and tabs from each line of
input, and to delete entirely blank lines.

```
#include  <stdio.h>
#define   MAXLINE   1000                /* maximum input line size */
#define   YES       1
#define   NO        0

main()                          /* trailing blanks and tabs remover */
{
    char line[MAXLINE];                 /* current input line      */

    while (getline(line, MAXLINE) > 0)
        if (remove(line) > 0)
            printf("%s\n", line);
}

remove(s)               /* remove trailing blanks and tabs in s */
char s[];
{
    int i;
    int nl;                             /* newline character flag */

    i = 0;
    while (s[i] != '\0')  /* find the end of character string s */
        ++i;
    --i;                    /* back off one position from '\0'    */
    if (s[i] == '\n') {
        nl = YES;
        --i;
    } else
        nl = NO;
    while (i >= 0 && (s[i] == ' ' || s[i] == '\t'))
        --i;
```

```
        if (i >= 0) {                   /* is it a nonblank line? */
            ++i;                        /* make room for '\0'     */
            if (nl == YES) {
                s[i] = '\n';
                ++i;
            }
            s[i] = '\0';
        }
        return(i);
}
```

The remove function removes trailing blanks and tabs from the character string line and returns its new length. If this length is greater than 0, line has characters other than blanks and tabs, and line is printed. Otherwise, line is entirely made up of blanks and tabs, and thus ignored. This ensures that entirely blank lines are not printed.

The remove function finds the end of string s and backs off one position from '\0' (end of string marker). If the character before '\0' is '\n', the newline flag (nl) is updated in order to preserve newlines in the output. The program then steps backwards over blanks and tabs until some other character is found or no more characters are available (i < 0).

If i >= 0 then there existed character(s) besides blanks and tabs. The newline is put back, if one existed, and the end of the string is marked with an '\0'. Regardless what i is, its value is returned by the function. The while loop repeats until an empty line is found (getline returns 0).

The function getline is the same as in Exercise 1-14.

Exercise 1-17: (page 28 K&R)

Write a function reverse(s) which reverses the character string s.
Use it to write a program which reverses its input a line at a time.

```c
#include   <stdio.h>
#define    MAXLINE   1000                    /* maximum input line size */

main()                     /* reverse the input a line at a time */
{
    char line[MAXLINE];                 /* current input line      */

    while (getline(line, MAXLINE) > 0) {
        reverse(line);
        printf("%s", line);
    }
}

reverse(s)                                       /* reverse string s */
char s[];
{
    int i, j;
    char temp;

    i = 0;                  /* find the end of character string s */
    while (s[i] != '\0')
        ++i;
    --i;                    /* back off one position from '\0'    */
    if (s[i] == '\n')
        --i;
    j = 0;                  /* beginning of character string s    */
    while (j < i) {
        temp = s[j];
        s[j] = s[i];                            /* swap the characters */
        s[i] = temp;
        --i;
        ++j;
    }
}
```

The reverse function first finds the end of string s. It backs off one position from '\0', so that the first character will not become an end of string marker. If a '\n' exists, it backs off one more position, since like the '\0', it must remain at the end of the line.

After the end of the string is found, j is the index of the first character of the string and i is the index of the last character of the string. While swapping characters, j is incremented (moves towards the end of the string), and i is decremented (moves towards the beginning of the string). The process continues while j is less than i.

The main program reads a line of input at a time, reverses it and prints the reversed line. The program continues until an empty line is found (getline(line, MAXLINE) == 0).

The function getline is the same as in Exercise 1-14.

reverse is rewritten in Exercise 5-4 using pointers (page 89 K&R). A version of reverse using recursion (page 84 K&R) is written in Exercise 4-9.

Exercise 1-18: (page 31 K&R)

The test in the for statement of getline above is rather ungainly. Rewrite the program to make it clearer, but retain the same behavior at end of file or buffer overflow. Is this behavior the most reasonable?

```
#include  <stdio.h>
#define   MAXLINE   1000              /* maximum input line size */
#define   YES       1
#define   NO        0

getline()                            /* rewritten version */
{
    int c, i, okloop;
    extern char line[];

    i = 0;
    okloop = YES;
    while (okloop == YES)
        if (i >= MAXLINE-1)
            okloop = NO;             /* buffer overflow */
        else {
            c = getchar();
            if (c == EOF || c == '\n')
                okloop = NO;         /* EOF or newline */
            else {
                line[i] = c;
                ++i;
            }
        }
}
```

The for loop is replaced by a while loop and an if-else statement. An integer boolean, okloop, controls the execution of the while loop. The loop is repeated as long as okloop equals YES.

The second part of the for statement, or the condition that controls the loop, is now an if-else statement. If any of the three conditions exist (i >= MAXLINE-1, c == EOF, c == '\n'), okloop is set equal to NO and the while loop terminates.

It is believed that this behavior is the most reasonable. Upon reaching an end of file or buffer overflow, the loop terminates.

Exercise 1-19:   (page 31 K&R)

Write a program `detab` which replaces tabs in the input with the proper number of blanks to space to the next tab stop. Assume a fixed set of tab stops, say every *n* positions.

```
#include  <stdio.h>
#define   TABINC    8                       /* tab increment size */

main()                              /* replace tabs with blanks */
{
     int c, nb, pos;

     nb = 0;                   /* number of blanks needed      */
     pos = 1;                  /* position of character in line */
     while ((c = getchar()) != EOF)
         if (c == '\t') {
              nb = TABINC - (pos - 1) % TABINC;   /* tab        */
              while (nb > 0) {
                   putchar(' ');
                   ++pos;
                   --nb;
              }
         } else if (c == '\n') {
              putchar(c);                          /* new line   */
              pos = 1;
         } else {
              putchar(c);                          /* all others */
              ++pos;
         }
}
```

The tab stops are every TABINC positions. In this program, TABINC is defined to be 8. The variable pos is the position within a line of text where the program currently is.

If the character is a tab, nb is calculated to determine how many blanks are needed to reach the next tab stop. The statement

```
nb = TABINC - (pos-1) % TABINC;
```

determines this value. If the character is a newline, then it is printed out and pos is reinitialized to the beginning of the line (pos = 1). Any other character is printed and pos is incremented (++pos).

The program detab is extended in Exercises 5-8 and 5-9.

Exercise 1-20: (page 31 K&R)

Write the program entab which replaces strings of blanks by the minimum number of tabs and blanks to achieve the same spacing. Use
the same tab stops as for detab.

```
#include  <stdio.h>
#define   TABINC   8                        /* tab increment size */

main()        /* replace strings of blanks with tabs and blanks */
{
    int c, nb, nt, pos;

    nb = 0;                                 /* # of blanks needed */
    nt = 0;                                 /* # of tabs needed   */
    for (pos = 1; (c = getchar()) != EOF; pos++)
        if (c == ' ')
            if (pos % TABINC != 0)
                ++nb;                        /* insert blank */
            else {
                nb = 0;          /* replace blanks with a tab */
                ++nt;
            }
        else {
            while (nt > 0) {                 /* output        */
                putchar('\t');
                --nt;
            }
            if (c != '\t')
                while (nb > 0) {
                    putchar(' ');
                    --nb;
                }
            else
                nb = 0;
            putchar(c);
            if (c == '\n')
                pos = 0;
            else if (c == '\t')
                pos = pos + (TABINC - (pos-1) % TABINC) - 1;
        }
}
```

The integer variables nb and nt are the minimum number of blanks and tabs needed to replace a string of blanks. The variable pos is the position within a line of text where the program currently is.

The idea is to find all blanks. A string of blanks is replaced by a tab if pos is a multiple of TABINC (pos % TABINC != 0 is false).

If a nonblank is found, then the accumulated tabs and blanks are printed followed by the character just found. nb and nt are now equal to 0, and a check is made to determine if a newline character is present. If so, pos is reset to the beginning of the new line.

If the nonblank found is a tab ('\t'), then only the accumulated tabs are printed followed by the tab just found.

The program entab is extended in Exercises 5-8 and 5-9.

Exercise 1-21: (page 31 K&R)

Write a program to "fold" long input lines after the last non-blank
character that occurs before the *n*-th column of input, where *n* is a
parameter. Make sure your program does something intelligent with
very long lines, and if there are no blanks or tabs before the specified
column.

```
#include   <stdio.h>
#define    MAXCOL    10                    /* max column of input */

int line[MAXCOL-1];                        /* line of input       */

main()                                     /* folds long input lines */
{
     int c, pos;

     pos = 1;                              /* position in line */
     while ((c = getchar()) != EOF) {
          line[pos-1] = c;                 /* store next char  */
          ++pos;
          if (pos >= MAXCOL) {
               pos = findnb(MAXCOL-2);     /* find non-blank   */
               printl(pos);
               pos = newpos(pos, MAXCOL-2);
          } else if (c == '\n') {
               printl(pos-1);
               pos = 1;
          }
     }
}

findnb(col)                    /* find position of last non-blank */
int col;                       /* starting at index col           */
{
     while (col >= 0 && (line[col] == ' ' || line[col] == '\t'))
          --col;
     return(col+1);
}
```

```
    newpos(i, col)                              /* find new position */
    int col, i;
    {
        int j, k;

        if (i > 0) {
            for (j = i, k = 0; j <= col; j++, k++)
                line[k] = line[j];
            return(k+1);
        } else
            return(1);
    }

    printl(pos)                                 /* print line */
    int pos;
    {
        int i;

        for (i = 0; i < pos; i++)
            putchar(line[i]);
        putchar('\n');
    }
```

MAXCOL is a symbolic constant. It indicates the n-th column of input. The integer variable pos is initialized to 1 and points to the position within a line of text where the program currently is. The program folds input lines before the n-th column of input.

When

```
    if (pos >= MAXCOL)
```

is true, the program is at column $n-1$ and the input line is folded.

The function findnb searches for a nonblank starting at the index col (MAXPOS-2 equals the last position in the line). It returns i+1 to conform with the printl function. Since the input line is folded at the last nonblank before the n-th column, it is necessary to move the blank(s) and/or tab(s) to the beginning of the line before the next character is read. This is the task of newpos. If i is greater than 0, then findnb found a nonblank. Whatever follows the last nonblank is moved to the beginning of the line:

```
for (j = i, k = 0; j <= col; j++, k++)
     line[k] = line[j];
```

If i is not greater than 0, then line contains only blank(s) and/or tab(s). The
new position (pos) is returned.

Exercise 1-22: (page 31 K&R)

Write a program to remove all comments from a C program. Don't
forget to handle quoted strings and character constants properly.

```
#include <stdio.h>

main()              /* remove all comments from a valid C program */
{
    int c, d;

    while ((c = getchar()) != EOF)
        if (c == '/')
            if ((d = getchar()) == '*')
                in_comment();              /* comment found */
            else {
                putchar(c);                /* no comment    */
                putchar(d);
            }
        else if (c == '\'' || c == '"')
            echo_quote(c);                 /* quote begins  */
        else
            putchar(c);                    /* no comment    */
}

in_comment()                        /* inside of a valid comment */
{
    int c, d;

    c = getchar();                          /* previous character */
    d = getchar();                          /* present character  */
    while (c != '*' || d != '/') {    /* search for comment end */
        c = d;
        d = getchar();
    }
}
```

```
echo_quote(c)                                  /* echo quote */
int c;
{
    int d;

    putchar(c);
    while ((d = getchar()) != c) {       /* search for quote end */
        putchar(d);
        if (d == '\\')
            putchar(getchar());          /* ignore escape seq    */
    }
    putchar(d);
}
```

The program assumes the input is a valid C program. The main routine searches for the beginning of a comment (/*) and if found, calls in_comment. This function searches for the comment end (*/). The procedure therefore ensures that a comment will be ignored.

The main routine also searches for single and double quotes and if found, calls echo_quote. The argument to echo_quote indicates whether it is a single or double quote. echo_quote is called to ensure that anything found within a quote is echoed and not mistaken for a comment. Any other character found is printed. echo_quote does not consider a quote following a backslash as the terminating quote (see the discussion on escape sequences on page 17 K&R and in Exercise 1-2).

The program terminates when getchar returns an end of file.

Exercise 1-23: (page 31 K&R)

Write a program to check a C program for rudimentary syntax errors
like unbalanced parentheses, brackets and braces. Don't forget about
quotes, both single and double, and comments. (This program is hard
if you do it in full generality.)

```c
#include <stdio.h>

int brace, brack, paren;

main()                                      /* basic syntax checker */
{
    int c;
    extern int brace, brack, paren;

    while ((c = getchar()) != EOF) {
        if (c == '/') {
            if ((c = getchar()) == '*')
                in_comment();               /* inside comment */
            else
                search(c);
        } else if (c == '\'' || c == '"')
            in_quote(c);                    /* inside quote   */
        else {
            search(c);
            if (brace < 0)                  /* output errors */
                printf("Unbalanced braces\n");
            if (brack < 0)
                printf("Unbalanced brackets\n");
            if (paren < 0)
                printf("Unbalanced parentheses\n");
        }
    }
    if (brace > 0)                          /* output errors */
        printf("Unbalanced braces\n");
    if (brack > 0)
        printf("Unbalanced brackets\n");
    if (paren > 0)
        printf("Unbalanced parentheses\n");
}
```

```
search(c)                    /* search for rudimentary syntax errors */
int c;
{
    extern int brace, brack, paren;

    if (c == '{')
        ++brace;
    else if (c == '}')
        --brace;
    else if (c == '[')
        ++brack;
    else if (c == ']')
        --brack;
    else if (c == '(')
        ++paren;
    else if (c == ')')
        --paren;
}

in_comment()                         /* inside of a valid comment */
{
    int c, d;

    c = getchar();                        /* previous character */
    d = getchar();                        /* present character  */
    while (c != '*' || d != '/') {    /* search for comment end */
        c = d;
        d = getchar();
    }
}

in_quote(c)                                       /* inside quote */
int c;
{
    int d;

    while ((d = getchar()) != c)          /* search for quote end */
        if (d == '\\')
            getchar();                    /* ignore escape seq   */
}
```

This solution is not done in full generality. The three syntax errors searched for are unbalanced parentheses, brackets, and braces. Everything else is assumed to be valid.

In the function search, the variable brace is incremented when a left brace ('{') is found and decremented when a right brace is found ('}'). The same occurs for the variable brack when a left bracket ('[') or a right bracket (']') is found, and for the variable paren when a left parenthesis ('(') or a right parenthesis (')') is found.

During the search, it is legal for brace, brack or paren to be positive or zero. It is an error if brace, brack or paren ever becomes negative; an appropriate message is printed. [[[(brack equals 3) is legal for the moment because 3 balancing right brackets might be found later in the search.]]] (brack equals -3) is illegal because there was no previous left brackets to balance these 3 right brackets; if there were 3 left brackets to balance them, then brack should equal 0. The statements

```
if (brace < 0)
    printf("Unbalanced braces\n");
if (brack < 0)
    printf("Unbalanced brackets\n");
if (paren < 0)
    printf("Unbalanced parentheses\n");
```

are needed because without them)(or]]][[[or }}{{ would be considered balanced.

The main routine searches for comments and single and double quotes. If one is found, then anything inside is simply ignored. The braces, brackets, and parentheses inside comments and quotes need not be balanced.

After all the text has been searched, a final check is made to determine if there are any open braces, brackets or parentheses. If so, an appropriate message is printed.

Exercise 2-1:   (page 39 K&R)

Write a loop equivalent to the for loop above without using &&.

Original:

```
for (i=0; i<lim-1 && (c=getchar()) != '\n' && c != EOF; ++i)
```

Equivalent:

```
for (i=0; !(!(i<lim-1) || !((c=getchar()) != '\n') || !(c != EOF));
     ++i)
```

The conditional expression in the original for loop is,

```
i<lim-1 && (c=getchar()) != '\n' && c != EOF
```

This expression is TRUE only when each of the three conditions is TRUE.

The && operator means AND. That is,

TRUE && TRUE && TRUE

yields TRUE. If any of the three conditions is FALSE, the result is FALSE.

The || operator means OR. The result of the || operator is FALSE only when each of the conditions is FALSE.

FALSE || FALSE || FALSE

yields FALSE.

Therefore, when each of the three conditions in the original for loop is negated and OR'ed,

```
!(i<lim-1) || !((c=getchar()) != '\n') || !(c != EOF)
```

the result is FALSE only when each condition is TRUE. Negating this final result yields TRUE, showing that the two for loops above are equivalent.

This solution can be taken one step further. The negation of each condition can be removed when the opposite of the original expression is tested. Another equivalent for loop is:

```
for (i=0; !(i>=lim-1 || (c=getchar()) == '\n' || c == EOF); ++i)
```

Exercise 2-2:   (page 42 K&R)

Write the function htoi(s), which converts a string of hexadecimal digits into its equivalent integer value. The allowable digits are 0 through 9, a through f, and A through F.

```
#define   YES      1
#define   NO       0

htoi(s)                  /* convert hexadecimal string s to integer */
char s[];
{
      int hexdigit, i, inhex, n;

      n = 0;                     /* integer value to be returned   */
      inhex = YES;               /* assume valid hexadecimal digit */
      for (i = 0; inhex == YES; i++) {
          if (s[i] >= '0' && s[i] <= '9')
              hexdigit = s[i] - '0';
          else if (s[i] >= 'a' && s[i] <= 'f')
              hexdigit = s[i] - 'a' + 10;
          else if (s[i] >= 'A' && s[i] <= 'F')
              hexdigit = s[i] - 'A' + 10;
          else
              inhex = NO;        /* not a valid hexadecimal digit */
          if (inhex == YES)
              n = 16 * n + hexdigit;
      }
      return(n);
}
```

The statement

```
    for (i = 0; inhex == YES; i++)
```

controls the function. The integer i is the index for the array s. While s[i] is a valid hexadecimal digit, inhex remains YES, and the loop continues. The variable hexdigit takes a numerical value of 0 through 15.

The statement

```
if (inhex == YES)
```

guarantees a valid hexadecimal digit was at `s[i]` and its value is in `hexdigit`. When the loop terminates, the calculated value (n) is returned.

This function is similar to `atoi` (page 39 K&R).

Exercise 2-3:   (page 44 K&R)

Write an alternate version of squeeze(s1, s2) which deletes each
character in s1 which matches any character in the string s2.

```
squeeze(s1, s2)           /* delete each char in s1 which is in s2 */
char s1[], s2[];
{
     int i, j, k;

     for (i = k = 0; s1[i] != '\0'; i++) {
          for (j = 0; s2[j] != '\0' && s2[j] != s1[i]; j++)
               ;
          if (s2[j] == '\0')            /* end of string - no match */
               s1[k++] = s1[i];
     }
     s1[k] = '\0';
}
```

The first statement,

```
for (i = k = 0; s1[i] != '\0'; i++)
```

initializes i and k, the indexes of s1 and the resulting string (also s1),
respectively. Each character in s1 which matches any character in s2 is
deleted. The loop continues until the end of the string s1.

The second for statement checks each character in s2 against the s1[i] character. This loop terminates when s2 runs out of characters or there is a
match. In the event that there is no match, s1[i] is copied to the resulting
string. If there is a match, the statement

```
if (s2[j] == '\0')
```

fails, and nothing is done to s1[i] — it is not copied to the resulting string
(it is squeezed out).

Exercise 2-4:   (page 44 K&R)

Write the function any(s1, s2) which returns the first location in the string s1 where any character from the string s2 occurs, or −1 if s1 contains no characters from s2.

```
any(s1, s2)                    /* return first location in s1 where */
char s1[], s2[];               /* any character from s2 occurs      */
{
    int i, j;

    for (i = 0; s1[i] != '\0'; i++) {
        for (j = 0; s2[j] != '\0' && s2[j] != s1[i]; j++)
            ;
        if (s2[j] == s1[i])        /* match found              */
            return(i);             /* location of first match  */
    }
    return(-1);                    /* s1 contains no chars from s2 */
}
```

The statement

```
    for (i = 0; s1[i] != '\0'; i++)
```

controls the loop. When the loop terminates normally (s1 runs out of characters), a −1 is returned to indicate that no character of s2 was found in s1.

The second for statement,

```
    for (j = 0; s2[j] != '\0' && s2[j] != s1[i]; j++)
        ;
```

is executed for each value of i. It compares each character of s2 with s1[i]. When the loop terminates due to a match (a character of s2 matches the character of s1 in the i-th position), the location of the match is returned.

Exercise 2-5:   (page 46 K&R)

Modify getbits to number bits from left to right.

```
getbits(x, p, n)                    /* get n bits from position p */
unsigned x, p, n;
{
    return(((x << (p+1-n)) & ~((unsigned)~0 >> n))
           >> (wordlength() - n));
}
```

The function getbits(x, p, n) returns, right adjusted, the n-bit field of x that begins at position p. The bits in x are numbered left to right. For illustration, let's assume x is eight bits long (the length of an unsigned integer is machine dependent), and it is set to some value:

```
0 1 2 3 4 5 6 7    bit positions
0 0 0 1 1 0 1 1    some value
```

Since n and p are sensible positive values, for example n = 2 and p = 3, the expression

```
x << (p+1-n)
```

becomes

```
x << (3+1-2)
x << (2)
```

It shifts x to the left so that the n-bit field becomes left justified

```
0 1 1 0 1 1 0 0
```

The expression

```
(unsigned) ~0 >> n
```

takes an unsigned integer of all ones and shifts them n positions to the right. This leaves an n-bit field of zeros at the left. A one's complement (˜) of this value produces an n-bit field of ones on the left and zeros everywhere else. A bitwise AND of this value and the shifted x, gives the n-bit field of x, starting at position p, left justified.

0	1	1	0	1	1	0	0	shifted x
1	1	0	0	0	0	0	0	value produced by the above expression
0	1	0	0	0	0	0	0	n-bit field left justified

If the answer requires the n-bit field to be right justified, then the n-bit field is to be shifted to the right by a new value: the number of bits in an unsigned integer minus n. The function wordlength returns the number of bits in an unsigned integer. wordlength is described in Exercise 2-6.

Exercise 2-6:   (page 46 K&R)

Write a function `wordlength()` which computes the word length of the host machine, that is, the number of bits in an `int`. The function should be portable, in the sense that the same source code works on all machines.

```
wordlength()       /* computes the word length of the host machine */
{
    int i;
    unsigned v = ~0;

    for (i = 1; (v = v >> 1) > 0; i++)
        ;
    return(i);
}
```

The unsigned integer variable v is initialized to all ones:

```
unsigned v = ~0;
```

The variable i counts how many right shifts are performed until v becomes all zeros.

v is shifted one position to the right, and this new value is assigned to v:

```
(v = v >> 1) > 0
```

The new value is then checked for greater than 0. If any bit position in v is still 1, the result is true. The loop continues until all bits in v have been shifted to the right; i has the number of shifts required and that is the word length.

Exercise 2-7:   (page 46 K&R)

Write the function `rightrot(n, b)` which rotates the integer n to the
right by b bit positions.

```
rightrot(n, b)                  /* rotate n to the right by b positions */
int n, b;
{
    int rbit;
    int lshift = wordlength() - 1;
    int clmbit = (unsigned) ~0 >> 1;

    while (b-- > 0) {
        rbit = n & 1;               /* get rightmost bit            */
        n = (n >> 1) & clmbit;      /* shift n 1 position right     */
                                    /* and clear leftmost bit       */
        rbit = rbit << lshift;      /* shift bit leftmost position  */
        n = n | rbit;               /* complete one rotation        */
    }
    return(n);
}
```

The variable `rbit` saves the rightmost bit of n. `lshift` is the left shift counter
for the rightmost bit, and `clmbit` (clear leftmost bit) is set to a field of all
ones shifted one position to the right (its leftmost bit is 0).

The statement,

```
n = (n >> 1) & clmbit;
```

shifts n to the right and clears the leftmost bit — this ensures that the sign
bit is not propagated on machines that do arithmetic right shifts. Next,

```
rbit = rbit << lshift;
```

moves the rightmost bit to the leftmost position. When this value is OR'ed
with the right shifted value of n, it completes one rotation. b rotations are
performed on n.

```
rightrot(n, b)
int n, b;
{
    int rbits;

    if ((b = b % wordlength()) > 0) {
        rbits = ~(~0 << b) & n; /* b rightmost bits of n          */
        n = n >> b;             /* n shifted b positions right */
        if (n < 0)              /* is n a negative number?     */
            n = n & ((unsigned) ~0 >> b);
                                /* clear propagated sign bit   */
        rbits = rbits << (wordlength() - b);
                                /* b rightmost bits to left    */
        n = n | rbits;          /* rotation completed          */
    }
    return(n);
}
```

This is a different solution to the same exercise. If the number of positions (b) to be rotated to the right is the same as the number of bits in an integer, nothing changes because n is the same as before the rotation. If b is less, only b positions need to be rotated. If b exceeds the number of bits in an integer, only the remainder of b divided by the length of the word (modulus operator) need to be rotated. As a result, no looping is necessary.

~0 << b   all ones are shifted b positions to the left
                 leaving b zeros on the rightmost positions.
~(~0 << b)   all ones are on the b rightmost positions.

When this value is bitwise AND'ed with n, the b rightmost bits of n are assigned to rbits. Now n can be shifted b positions to the right. If n is a negative number, the sign bit may have been propagated on machines that do arithmetic right shifts and needs to be cleared. rbits are then moved to the leftmost position. This value is OR'ed with the right shifted value of n to complete the rotation of the integer n, b positions to the right.

Exercise 2-8:   (page 46 K&R)

Write the function invert(x, p, n) which inverts (i.e., changes 1 into 0 and vice versa) the n bits of x that begin at position p, leaving the others unchanged.

```
invert(x, p, n)     /* inverts n bits of x beginning at position p */
unsigned x, p, n;
{
    return(x ^ (~(~0 << n) << (p+1-n)));
}
```

First,

```
(~0 << n)
```

shifts all ones n positions to the left, leaving n zeros at the rightmost positions.

Second,

```
~(~0 << n)
```

places all ones at the rightmost positions, zeros everywhere else.

Third,

```
(~(~0 << n) << (p+1-n))
```

shifts these n 1-bits to position p.

Finally,

```
x ^ (~(~0 << n) << (p+1-n))
```

the bitwise exclusive OR operator (^) produces a 1 when two bits are different, otherwise it produces a 0. Since the objective is to invert the n bits starting at position p, it suffices to exclusive OR them with all ones starting at p for n bits (with zeros everywhere else). If the original bit is 0 exclusive OR with a 1, it produces a 1 — it was inverted. If the original bit is a 1 exclusive OR with a 1, it produces a 0 — it was inverted.

The positions outside of the n bit field are exclusive OR'ed with zeros: 0 ^ 0 (bits are the same) produces a 0 — nothing changed; 1 ^ 0 (bits are different) produces a 1 — nothing changed. Only the n bits are inverted.

Exercise 2-9:   (page 47 K&R)

In a 2's complement number system, x & (x-1) deletes the rightmost 1-bit in x. (Why?) Use this observation to write a faster version of bitcount.

```
bitcount(n)                     /* count 1 bits in n  -  faster version */
unsigned n;
{
    int b;

    for (b = 0; n != 0; n &= n-1)
        ++b;
    return(b);
}
```

Take a value for x-1, for example the binary number 1010, which is 10 in decimal. (x-1) + 1 produces x:

binary		decimal
1010	$x-1$	10
+ 1		+ 1
————		————
1011	x	11

In binary, one of the consequences of the addition is that the rightmost 0-bit of x-1 changes to 1 in the result x. Therefore, the rightmost 1-bit of x has a corresponding 0-bit in x-1. This is why x & (x-1), in a 2's complement number system, will delete the rightmost 1-bit in x.

Consider an unsigned quantity of four bits. To count all 1-bits in this quantity, the original bitcount performs four shifts to check the rightmost bit. An alternative is to use the knowledge that x & (x-1) turns off the rightmost 1-bit of x. For example, if x equals 9,

1	0	0	1	value 9 in binary (x)
1	0	0	0	value 8 $(x-1)$
1	0	0	0	x & $(x-1)$

and the rightmost 1-bit in x has been deleted. The resulting value is 1000 in binary, 8 in decimal. Repeating the process,

```
1  0  0  0    value 8 in binary (x)
0  1  1  1    value 7 (x−1)
0  0  0  0    x & (x−1)
```

and the rightmost 1-bit in x has been deleted. The resulting value is 0000 in binary, 0 in decimal. There are no more 1-bits in x and the process terminates.

The worst case is when all bits of x are ones — the number of AND's is the same as the number of shifts in bitcount. Overall, this is a faster version.

Exercise 2-10: (page 48 K&R)

Rewrite the function `lower`, which converts upper case letters to lower case, with a conditional expression instead of `if-else`.

```
lower(c)                    /* convert c to lower case: ASCII only */
int c;
{
    return(c >= 'A' && c <= 'Z' ? c + 'a' - 'A' : c);
}
```

When the condition

```
c >= 'A' && c <= 'Z'
```

is true, c is an upper case letter (ASCII only). Then the expression

```
c + 'a' - 'A'
```

is evaluated and a lower case letter is returned. Otherwise, the character is returned unchanged.

Exercise 3-1:   (page 56 K&R)

Write a function expand(s, t) which converts characters like newline
and tab into visible escape sequences like \n and \t as it copies the
string s to t. Use a switch.

```
expand(s, t)    /* expand newline and tab into visible sequences  */
char s[], t[];
{
    int i, j;

    for (i = j = 0; s[i] != '\0'; i++)
        switch (s[i]) {
        case '\n':                      /* newline                 */
            t[j++] = '\\';
            t[j++] = 'n';
            break;
        case '\t':                      /* tab                     */
            t[j++] = '\\';
            t[j++] = 't';
            break;
        default:                        /* all other characters    */
            t[j++] = s[i];
            break;
        }
    t[j] = '\0';
}
```

The statement

```
for (i = j = 0; s[i] != '\0'; i++)
```

controls the loop. The variable i is the index for the original string s and j is the index for copied and modified string t.

There are three cases in the switch statement: '\n' for newline character, '\t' for tab character, and default. If the character s[i] does not match one of the two cases, the case labeled default is executed: s[i] is just copied to string t.

Exercise 3-2:   (page 59 K&R)

Write a function expand(s1, s2) which expands short-hand notations like a-z in the string s1 into the equivalent complete list abc...xyz in s2. Allow for letters of either case and digits, and be prepared to handle cases like a-b-c and a-z0-9 and -a-z. (A useful convention is that a leading or trailing - is taken literally.)

```
expand(s1, s2)                      /* expand short-hand notations   */
char s1[], s2[];
{
    int err, i, j, last;
    int from, to;

    err = 0;                        /* no error found        */
    j = 0;                          /* index of expanded str */
    last = strlen(s1) - 1;          /* index of last position*/
    for (i = 0; i <= last; i++) {
        if (s1[i] == '-')           /* it is a -             */
            if (i == 0 || i == last) /* leading or trailing - */
                from = to = '-';
            else if (to != '-') {    /* a-b-c  case          */
                from = to + 1;
                if (s1[i+1] != '-')  /* avoid two - in a row  */
                    to = s1[++i];
                else {
                    to = -1;         /* remember error        */
                    ++i;             /* ignore short-hand     */
                }
            } else {                /* last char was a -     */
                to = -1;            /* remember error        */
                ++i;
            }
        else {                      /* it is not a -         */
            from = s1[i];
            if (i+2 > last )        /* not enough characters */
                to = -1;
            else if (s1[i+1] != '-') /* a - was expected      */
                to = -1;
            else if (s1[i+2] == '-') /* avoid two - in a row  */
                to = -1;
```

```
                else {                      /* seems valid short-hand*/
                        i += 2;
                        to = s1[i];
                }
        }
        if (from > to)                       /* any error found ?      */
                err = -1;
        else                                 /* expand short-hand      */
                for ( ; from <= to; from++)
                        s2[j++] = from;
    }
    s2[j] = '\0';
    return(err);
}
```

The function strlen returns the length of a character string (page 36 K&R).
The index of the last character of the string is the length of the string minus
1:

```
    last = strlen(s1) - 1;
```

The current character s1[i] can be a '-'. If the '-' is the first or the last
character in the string it is taken literally:

```
    if (i == 0 || i == last)
        from = to = '-';
```

If it is not the first or last character, the preceding character is checked to
avoid two −'s in a row:

```
    else if (to != '-')
```

This happens in a string like a-b-c after a-b has been recognized. The
statement

```
    if (s1[i+1] != '-')
```

again checks for two −'s in a row to avoid invalid short-hand like a-b--c.

The other possibility is that the current character is not a '-'. In this case at
least two more characters are needed: a '-' followed by some other character. If the next character is not a '-', it is an error:

```
    else if (s1[i+1] != '-')
        to = -1;
```

If the third character is not a `'-'`, a sequence as in a-z was found.

The variables from and to contain the characters for the short-hand notation. It is an error for the value of the variable from to be bigger than the value of the variable to (as in z-a).

When the notation is valid it is expanded in s2:

```
    for ( ; from <= to; from++)
        s2[j++] = from;
```

If an error is detected anywhere in the notation the variable to is set to −1. This value is always less than the value in the variable from and the current short-hand is ignored. The variable err is then set to −1 to remember the error; if no error occurs, err is set to 0. The variable err is returned to indicate failure or success.

The statement of the problem mentions letters and numbers. The alternatives are to make the program expand letters, numbers, and −'s, or to make it expand arbitrary characters. Since it is easier to expand arbitrary characters (it includes letters, numbers, and −'s) this solution follows the second alternative. The function expand works for ASCII characters. The short-hand a-z expands into the equivalent list abc...xyz. The short-hand !-˜ expands into !"#..ABC..XYZ..abc..xyz..|}˜ which is something big.

Exercise 3-3:   (page 60 K&R)

In a 2's complement number representation, our version of itoa does not handle the largest negative number, that is, the value of *n* equal to $-(2^{wordsize-1})$. Explain why not. Modify it to print that value correctly, regardless of the machine it runs on.

```
#define   abs(x)    ((x) < 0 ? -(x) : (x))

itoa(n, s)      /* convert n to characters in s - modified      */
char s[];
int n;
{
    int i, sign;

    sign = n;             /* record sign                        */
    i = 0;
    do {                  /* generate digits in reverse order   */
        s[i++] = abs(n % 10) + '0';   /* get next digit         */
    } while ((n /= 10) != 0);         /* delete it              */
    if (sign < 0)
        s[i++] = '-';
    s[i] = '\0';
    reverse(s);
}
```

$$-(2^{wordsize-1})$$

cannot be converted to a positive number as in

```
n = -n;
```

because the largest positive number in a 2's complement representation is:

$$2^{wordsize-1} - 1$$

The variable sign saves the initial value of n. The macro abs finds the absolute value of n % 10. This avoids the

$$-(2^{wordsize-1})$$

problem because only the result of the modulus operator is made positive. The conditional expression in the do-while statement has been changed from

    (n /= 10) > 0

to

    (n /= 10) != 0

because if n is negative it remains negative during the execution of itoa.

Exercise 3-4:   (page 60 K&R)

Write the analogous function itob(n, s) which converts the unsigned integer n into a binary character representation in s. Write itoh, which converts an integer to hexadecimal representation.

```
itob(n, s)              /* convert n to characters in s - binary   */
char s[];
unsigned n;
{
    int i;

    i = 0;
    do {                    /* generate digits in reverse order   */
        s[i++] = n % 2 + '0';                /* get next digit   */
    } while ((n /= 2) != 0);                 /* delete it        */
    s[i] = '\0';
    reverse(s);
}
```

Since n is unsigned, there is no sign to record. The contents of n are converted to binary so

    n % 2

returns either 0 or 1, and

    n /= 2

deletes that number from n. The iteration continues while n/2 is not 0.

```
itoh(n, s)        /* convert n to characters in s - hexadecimal     */
char s[];
unsigned n;
{
    int h, i;

    i = 0;
    do {                             /* generate digits in reverse */
        h = n % 16;                            /* get next digit    */
        s[i++] = (h <= 9) ? h+'0' : h+'a'-10;
    } while ((n /= 16) != 0);                  /* delete it         */
    s[i] = '\0';
    reverse(s);
}
```

The function itoh is similar to itob in the first part of this exercise. One difference is that

```
h = n % 16;
```

returns a value between 0 and 15 inclusive.

The statement

```
s[i++] = (h <= 9) ? h+'0' : h+'a'-10;
```

returns a hexadecimal character. If h is less than or equal to 9, then the ASCII character is

```
h+'0'
```

Otherwise,

```
h+'a'-10
```

produces a lower case letter between a and f that represents a value between 10 and 15 inclusive.

Exercise 3-5:   (page 60 K&R)

Write a version of itoa which accepts three arguments instead of
two. The third argument is a minimum field width; the converted
number must be padded with blanks on the left if necessary to make
it wide enough.

```
#define   abs(x)    ((x) < 0 ? -(x) : (x))

itoa(n, s, w)  /* convert n to characters in s, w characters wide*/
char s[];
int n, w;
{
    int i, sign;

    sign = n;           /* record sign                            */
    i = 0;
    do {                /* generate digits in reverse order       */
        s[i++] = abs(n % 10) + '0';      /* get next digit        */
    } while ((n /= 10) != 0);            /* delete it             */
    if (sign < 0)
        s[i++] = '-';
    while (i < w)       /* pad with blanks while there is room    */
        s[i++] = ' ';
    s[i] = '\0';
    reverse(s);
}
```

This function is similar to itoa in Exercise 3-3. The necessary modification is

```
while (i < w)
    s[i++] = ' ';
```

The while loop pads the string s with blanks if necessary.

Exercise 3-6:   (page 62 K&R)

Write a program which copies its input to its output, except that it
prints only one instance from each group of adjacent identical lines.
(This is a simple version of the UNIX utility uniq.)

```
#include   <stdio.h>
#define    MAXLINE   100

main()              /* eliminate identical adjacent lines - uniq */
{
    char line[MAXLINE];             /* current input line   */
    char lastline[MAXLINE];         /* last input line      */

    lastline[0] = '\0';
    while (getline(line, MAXLINE) > 0)
        if (strcmp(line, lastline) != 0) {
            printf("%s\n", line);
            copy(line, lastline);
        }
}
```

The function getline is the one used in Exercise 1-14.

The string lastline remembers the last line read. When the program begins
lastline is empty. strcmp compares two character strings and returns 0 if
the strings are equal. strcmp is described on page 101 K&R, and the function
copy on page 26 K&R.

```
#include   <stdio.h>
#define    MAXLINE   100

main()                    /* eliminate identical adjacent lines - uniq */
{
    char line[MAXLINE];                    /* current input line    */
    char lastline[MAXLINE];                /* last input line       */

    lastline[0] = '\0';
    while (getline(line, MAXLINE) > 0) {
        if (strcmp(line, lastline) == 0)
            continue;
        printf("%s\n", line);
        copy(line, lastline);
    }
}
```

This solution uses the continue statement. When the character strings line
and lastline are equal the program continues with the test part of the while
statement:

```
if (strcmp(line, lastline) == 0)
    continue;
```

Otherwise, printf and copy are executed and only then the while statement
is executed again.

Exercise 4-1: (page 68 K&R)

Write the function rindex(s, t), which returns the position of the rightmost occurrence of t in s, or −1 if there is none.

```
rindex(s, t)     /* returns rightmost index of t in s, -1 if none */
char s[], t[];
{
    int i, j, k, pos;

    pos = -1;                            /* index of t in s */

    for (i = 0; s[i] != '\0'; i++) {
        for (j=i, k=0; t[k]!='\0' && s[j]==t[k]; j++, k++)
            ;
        if (t[k] == '\0')
            pos = i;
    }
    return(pos);
}
```

rindex is similar to the routine index (page 67 K&R). When a match is found in index, the position of the first element of t within s is returned to the calling program. However, in rindex, this position is stored in the variable pos,

```
if (t[k] == '\0')
    pos = i;
```

and the search continues at s[i+1]. Finally, when the array s has been completely searched (s[i] is '\0'), the position of the rightmost occurrence of t in s is returned.

Exercise 4-2:   (page 71 K&R)

Extend atof so it handles scientific notation of the form

    123.45e − 6

where a floating point number may be followed by e or E and an
optionally signed exponent.

```
double atof(s)                      /* convert string s to double  */
char s[];                           /* handles scientific notation */
{
    double val, power;
    int exp, i, sign;

    for (i=0; s[i]==' ' || s[i]=='\n' || s[i]=='\t'; i++)
        ;                                   /* skip white space */
    sign = 1;
    if (s[i] == '+' || s[i] == '-')             /* sign             */
        sign = (s[i++] == '+') ? 1 : -1;
    for (val = 0; s[i] >= '0' && s[i] <= '9'; i++)
        val = 10 * val + s[i] - '0';        /* integer part     */
    if (s[i] == '.')
        i++;
    for (power = 1; s[i] >= '0' && s[i] <= '9'; i++) {
        val = 10 * val + s[i] - '0';        /* fractional part  */
        power *= 10;
    }
    val = sign * val / power;

    if (s[i] == 'e' || s[i] == 'E') {
        i++;                                /* scientific notation */
        sign = 1;
        if (s[i] == '+' || s[i] == '-')
            sign = (s[i++] == '+') ? 1 : -1;
        for (exp = 0; s[i] >= '0' && s[i] <= '9'; i++)
            exp = 10 * exp + s[i] - '0';
```

```
            if (sign == 1)
                while (exp-- > 0)            /* positive exponent   */
                    val *= 10;
            else
                while (exp-- > 0)            /* negative exponent   */
                    val /= 10;
    }
    return(val);
}
```

The integer variable exp contains the absolute value of the exponent. The variable sign first contains the sign of the mantissa and then the sign of the exponent, if one exists. The double variable power is 10 raised to the number of digits to the right of the decimal point. The double variable val is at first the value of the mantissa and then the value of the double number (mantissa and exponent).

The first half of the routine is a duplication of atof (page 69 K&R). White spaces are skipped, the sign is recorded, and the double number (mantissa) is stored in the variable val. However, instead of immediately returning the result, (sign * val / power), this value is stored in the variable val.

The second half of the program handles the optional exponent. If an exponent does not exist then the number stored in val is returned to the calling program. If the exponent exists then the sign of the exponent gets stored in the variable sign and the value of the exponent gets calculated and stored in exp.

The final operation

```
    if (sign == 1)
        while (exp-- > 0)
            val *= 10;
    else
        while (exp-- > 0)
            val /= 10;
```

adjusts the mantissa according to the value of the exponent. If the exponent is positive, the mantissa is multiplied by 10 exp times. If the exponent is negative, the mantissa gets divided by 10 exp times. val then contains the final number which is returned to the calling program.

val is divided by 10 rather than multiplied by 0.1, since 0.1 is not an exact fraction in binary. In most machines, 0.1 is represented as slightly less than 0.1 and therefore 10.0 times 0.1 is rarely 1.0. Repeated division by 10 is better than repeated multiplication by 0.1, however in the former there is still a loss of accuracy.

Exercise 4-3: (page 76 K&R)

Given the basic framework, it's straightforward to extend the
calculator. Add the modulus (%) and unary minus operators. Add an
"erase" command which erases the top entry on the stack. Add com-
mands for handling variables. (Twenty-six single-letter variable names
is easy.)

```c
#include  <stdio.h>

#define MAXOP      20        /* max size of operand, operator */
#define NUMBER    '0'        /* signal that number found      */
#define TOOBIG    '9'        /* signal that string is too big */

double storage[26];        /* values of 26 variable names (A-Z) */

main()                     /* reverse Polish desk calculator */
{
    int type, var = 0;
    char s[MAXOP];
    double op2, atof(), pop(), push();

    while ((type = getop(s, MAXOP)) != EOF) {
        switch (type) {
        case NUMBER:
            push(atof(s));
            break;
        case '+':
            push(pop() + pop());
            break;
        case '*':
            push(pop() * pop());
            break;
        case '-':
            op2 = pop();
            push(pop() - op2);
            break;
```

```
case '/':
    op2 = pop();
    if (op2 != 0.0)
        push(pop() / op2);
    else
        printf("zero divisor popped\n");
    break;
case '%':                           /* modulus       */
    op2 = pop();
    if (op2 != 0.0)
        push((double) ((int)pop() % (int)op2));
    else
        printf("zero divisor popped\n");
    break;
case '=':
    printf("\t%f\n", push(pop()));
    break;
case 'c':                           /* clear stack   */
    clear();
    break;
case 'e':                           /* erase top entry */
    erase();
    break;
case 'm':                           /* unary minus   */
    push(-pop());
    break;
case 's':                           /* storage       */
    if (var >= 'A' && var <= 'Z') {
        pop();
        storage[var - 'A'] = pop();
    } else
        printf("no variable to store\n");
    break;
case TOOBIG:
    printf("%.20s ... is too long\n", s);
    break;
```

```
                default:
                    if (type >= 'A' && type <= 'Z')
                        push(storage[type - 'A']);
                    else
                        printf("unknown command %c\n", type);
                    break;
                }
                var = type;                              /* reset var */
        }
    }

    erase()                             /* erase top entry on stack */
    {
        extern int sp;                         /* stack pointer */
        if (sp > 0)
            --sp;
        else {
            printf("error: stack empty\n");
            clear();
        }
    }
```

Modifications are made to the main routine only. The routines push, pop, and clear (page 75 K&R) are unchanged.

The modulus operator (%) is handled similarly to the division operator (/). The modulus operation

```
op2 = pop();
if (op2 != 0.0)
    push((double) ((int)pop() % (int)op2));
```

is performed on the top two elements on the stack. op2 is the top element on the stack and is checked for a value of 0.0 before the modulus operation is performed. Since the modulus operator cannot be applied to double variables, the two operands are converted to integers through casts (page 42 K&R). The result of the modulus operation is then converted to a double, also through a cast.

The unary minus operator (m) pops the top element on the stack, changes its sign, and pushes the result back on the stack:

```
push(-pop());
```

The erase command (e) invokes the routine erase. erase decrements the stack pointer by 1 or produces an error message if the stack is empty.

A variable is any of the 26 upper case letters (A-Z). The double array storage allocates 26 double words. The contents of the variable A are stored in storage[0] and the contents of Z are stored in storage[25]. Since storage is declared external (page 37 K&R), by default each element is initialized to 0.0.

If a variable name (A-Z) is fetched from input the contents of the appropriate element of storage is pushed on the stack:

```
if (type >= 'A' && type <= 'Z')
    push(storage[type - 'A']);
```

Any operation can be performed on a variable (A-Z). For example, if A is equal to 5, then the addition operation

```
6 A + =
```

adds 6 to A which produces 11. The store operation (s) can also be performed on variables. This operation assigns to a variable the next to the top element on the stack:

```
pop();
storage[var - 'A'] = pop();
```

For example, to assign 5 to the variable B, the command would be,

```
5 B s
```

The effect of the store command (s) would be to pop B, pop 5, and store 5 in storage[1] (B).

The variable var is equal to the type of the previous operand/operator. It gets reset each time an operand/operator is fetched:

```
var = type;
```

The purpose of var is to determine whether the last element fetched was a variable name (A-Z). The store command uses this information to determine if a variable name has been specified:

```
if (var >= 'A' && var <= 'Z')
```

If one has not been specified then an error message is produced.

Exercise 4-4:   (page 79 K&R)

Write a routine ungets(s) which will push back an entire string onto
the input. Should ungets know about buf and bufp, or should it just
use ungetch?

```
ungets(s)                               /* push string back on input */
char s[];
{
      int len = strlen(s);              /* length of string s */

      while (len > 0)
          ungetch(s[--len]);
}
```

The variable len contains the number of characters in the string s (excluding
the terminating '\0'), which is determined by the function strlen (page 36
K&R).

The routine ungetch (page 79 K&R) is called len times, each time pushing
back a character from the string s onto the input. The last character in s
(s[len-1]) is pushed back first and the first character in s (s[0]) is pushed
back last.

ungets is simplified by using the routine ungetch. The character array buf
and the integer variable bufp need not be known to ungets. The routine
ungetch will handle buf, bufp, and the error checking.

Exercise 4-5: (page 79 K&R)

Suppose that there will never be more than one character of pushback. Modify getch and ungetch accordingly.

```
#include  <stdio.h>

int buf;                /* buffer for ungetch              */
                        /* handles EOF in a portable way   */
int bufp = 0;           /* 0 if buffer empty, 1 if buffer occupied */

getch()                 /* get a (possibly pushed back) character */
{
    if (bufp == 1) {
        bufp = 0;
        return(buf);                    /* set buffer empty */
    } else
        return(getchar());
}

ungetch(c)              /* push character back on input */
int c;
{
    if (bufp == 0) {
        bufp = 1;
        buf = c;
    } else
        printf("ungetch: too many characters\n");
}
```

The buffer, buf, is no longer declared an array because there will never be more than 1 character in the buffer at any time. buf is declared an integer rather than a character in order to handle a pushed-back EOF in a portable way (Exercise 4-6).

The integer variable bufp determines whether the buffer is empty or occupied. bufp is equal to 0 when the buffer is empty and bufp is equal to 1 when the buffer is occupied.

The routine getch tests if bufp equals 1. If bufp is 1, then bufp is set equal to 0 and the contents of the buffer is returned. Otherwise, the value obtained by getchar is returned to the calling routine.

The routine ungetch tests if bufp equals 0. If bufp is 0 then bufp is set equal to 1 and c is stored in the buffer. Otherwise, an error message is printed.

Exercise 4-6:   (page 80 K&R)

Our getch and ungetch do not handle a pushed-back EOF in a portable way. Decide what their properties ought to be if an EOF is pushed back, then implement your design.

```
#include  <stdio.h>
#define   BUFSIZE   100

int buf[BUFSIZE];              /* buffer for ungetch        */
                               /* handles EOF in a portable way */
int bufp = 0;                  /* next free position in buf */

getch()                /* get a (possibly pushed back) character */
{
    return((bufp > 0) ? buf[--bufp] : getchar());
}

ungetch(c)                     /* push a character back on input */
int c;
{
    if (bufp > BUFSIZE)
        printf("ungetch: too many characters\n");
    else
        buf[bufp++] = c;
}
```

In the header file, stdio.h (page 143 K&R), the symbolic constant EOF may be defined to be −1:

```
#define EOF (-1)
```

In the routines getch and ungetch (page 79 K&R), the buffer, buf, is declared to be an array of characters:

```
char buf[BUFSIZE];
```

The C Programming Language does not require a char variable to be signed or unsigned (page 40 K&R). When a char is converted to an int, it might never produce a negative number. On some computers, if the leftmost bit of a char is 1, it will produce a negative number when converted to an int. On other computers, a char is converted to an int by adding zeros at the left end. This conversion will always produce a positive number, regardless of whether the leftmost bit was 1 or not.

In hexadecimal notation -1 is 0xFFFF. When a 0xFFFF is stored in a char, the actual number being stored is 0xFF. When 0xFF is converted to an int, it might produce 0x00FF, which is 255, or 0xFFFF, which is -1.

negative number (-1)	→	character	→	integer
0xFFFF		0xFF		0x00FF (255)
0xFFFF		0xFF		0xFFFF (-1)

To guarantee portability, the buffer, buf, should be declared an array of integers:

```
int buf[BUFSIZE];
```

No conversions will occur and EOF (-1) or any negative number will be handled in a portable way.

Exercise 4-7: (page 85 K&R)

Adapt the ideas of printd to write a recursive version of itoa; that is, convert an integer into a string with a recursive routine.

```
itoa(n, s)              /* convert n to characters in s (recursive) */
char s[];
int n;
{
    int sign;

    sign = (n < 0) ? -1 : 1;
    n = (n < 0) ? -n : n;
    itoar(n, s, 0, sign);
}

itoar(n, s, j, sign)
char s[];
int j, n, sign;
{
    int i;

    if ((i = n/10) != 0) {
        s[j++] = n % 10 + '0';
        itoar(i, s, j, sign);
    }

    if (i == 0) {
        s[j++] = n % 10 + '0';
        if (sign < 0)
            s[j++] = '-';
        s[j] = '\0';
        reverse(s);
    }
}
```

The same user interface to the routine itoa must be maintained regardless of implementation. Therefore, only the number and the character string are passed to itoa.

With the language constructs known up to this exercise, the solution is awkward. itoa determines the sign of the number and then calls another routine
itoar which performs the conversion.

Four parameters are passed to the recursive routine itoar. n is the number to
be converted. It is converted a digit at a time beginning at its rightmost digit.
s is the string and j is the current position in the string. Initially j is set
equal to 0. sign, which is determined in itoa, contains −1 if the number to
be converted is negative and 1 if the number is positive.

The routine itoar consists of two if statements.

The first if statement

```
if ((i = n/10) != 0)
```

removes the rightmost digit from n and stores the remaining number in i.
For example,

```
n = 120  n/10 = 120/10 = 12   remove 0   i = 12
n =   9  n/10 =   9/10 =  0   remove 9   i =  0
```

If i is nonzero (there is one or more digits left) then the body of the first if
statement is executed. The rightmost digit of n is converted to its ASCII
value, stored in the string s, j is incremented and itoar is called with i as
the number to be converted.

If i is zero, the body of the second if statement is executed. n, which finally
contains only one digit, is converted to its ASCII value and stored in s. The
sign, if negative, is appended to s and the string s is reversed (reverse(s),
page 59 K&R). s[0] now contains either the leftmost digit of n or a negative
sign.

The unary operator & which gives the address of an object is not presented until page 89 K&R. With that knowledge the solution could be:

```
itoa(n, s)              /* convert n to characters in s - recursive  */
char s[];
int n;
{
    int j, power;
    int i = 0;

    if (n < 0) {
        s[i++] = '-';                        /* sign               */
        n = -n;                              /* make n positive    */
    }
    power = 1;
    for (j = n; j / 10 != 0; j /= 10)        /* generate digits    */
        power *= 10;                         /* in correct order   */
    s[i++] = j + '0';

    if (n / 10 != 0)
        itoa(n-j*power, &s[i]);              /* get next digit     */
    else
        s[i] = '\0';
}
```

Exercise 4-8:   (page 86 K&R)

Write a recursive version of the function reverse(s), which reverses
the string s.

```
reverse(s)                    /* reverse string s in place (recursive) */
char s[];
{
    reverser(s, 0, strlen(s));
}

reverser(s, i, len)
char s[];
int i;                        /* left pointer to string  */
int len;                      /* length of string        */
{
    int c, j;

    j = len - (i + 1);        /* right pointer to string */

    if (i < j) {
        c = s[i];
        s[i] = s[j];
        s[j] = c;
        reverser(s, ++i, len);
    }
}
```

The same user interface to the routine reverse must be maintained regardless
of implementation. Therefore, only the character string is passed to reverse.

With the language constructs known up to this exercise, the solution is awkward. reverse determines the length of the string and then calls reverser
which performs the reversal.

Three parameters are passed to reverser. s is the string to be reversed, i is
the left-side pointer to the string and len is the length of the string
(strlen(s), page 36 K&R). Initially, i is equal to 0.

j is the right-side pointer to the string. j is computed as

```
j = len - (i + 1);
```

The characters in the string are swapped from the outside in. For example, the first two characters swapped are s[0] and s[len-1] and the second two characters swapped are s[1] and s[len-2]. The left-side pointer, i, is incremented by 1, every time reverser is called:

```
reverser(s, ++i, len);
```

The swapping continues until either the two pointers are pointing to the same characters (i == j) or the left-side pointer points to a character to the right of the right-side pointer (i > j).

Pointers are not presented until page 89 K&R. With that knowledge the solution could be:

```
reverse(s)                  /* reverse string s in place (recursive) */
char s[];
{
    reverser(s, s + strlen(s) - 1);
}

reverser(s, t)
char *s;                     /* left-side pointer to string  */
char *t;                     /* right-side pointer to string */
{
    int c;

    if (s < t) {
        c = *s;
        *s = *t;
        *t = c;
        reverser(++s, --t);
    }
}
```

The solution is still awkward but better than the first solution because one less argument is passed to reverser and pointers are used instead of indexing.

Initially, s points to the first character in the string and t points to the last character in the string (excluding the terminating '\0').

The logic of reverser is similar to the first solution.

Exercise 4-9:   (page 87 K&R)

Define a macro swap(x, y) which interchanges its two int arguments. (Block structure will help.)

```
#define swap(x, y) { int __z; __z = y; y = x; x = __z; }
```

The swap macro works if neither of the arguments is __z. If one of the arguments has the name __z, then when the macro is expanded it becomes

```
{ int __z; __z = __z; __z = x; x = __z; }
```

and the result is undefined. The assumption made is that __z will not be used
as a variable name.

```
#define swap(x, y) { x ^= y; y ^= x; x ^= y; }
```

This solution uses the bitwise exclusive OR operator (^). The following table
shows the resulting value of z for different values of x and y:

x	^	y	=	z
0		0		0
0		1		1
1		0		1
1		1		0

x and y are swapped by exclusive OR'ing x and y three times:

```
x = x ^ y;
y = x ^ y;
x = x ^ y;
```

The first exclusive OR operation sets x equal to a mask. A bit in this mask is
equal to 1 if both bits in the original x and the original y differ, and a bit is
equal to 0 if both bits in the original x and the original y are equal. The second exclusive OR operation sets y equal to the original x from the information in the mask and from the original y. The third exclusive OR operation
sets x equal to the original y from the information in the mask and from the
new y (original x).

Exercise 5-1: (page 93 K&R)

Write getfloat, the floating point analog of getint. What type does getfloat return as its function value?

```
#include  <stdio.h>

getfloat(pn)           /* get next floating point number from input */
float *pn;
{
    int c, sign;
    float power;

    while ((c = getch()) == ' ' || c == '\n' || c == '\t')
        ;                              /* skip white space */
    sign = 1;
    if (c == '+' || c == '-') {            /* record sign      */
        sign = (c == '+') ? 1 : -1;
        c = getch();
    }
    for (*pn = 0.0; c >= '0' && c <= '9'; c = getch())
        *pn = 10.0 * *pn + c - '0';        /* integer part     */
    if (c == '.')
        c = getch();
    for (power = 1.0; c >= '0' && c <= '9'; c = getch()) {
        *pn = 10.0 * *pn + c - '0';        /* fractional part */
        power *= 10.0;
    }
    *pn *= sign / power;                    /* final number     */
```

```
    if (c != EOF)
        ungetch(c);
    return(c);
}
```

The routine getfloat is similar to the routine getint (page 93 K&R). getfloat skips white spaces, records the sign and stores the integer part of the number at the location pointed to by pn.

getfloat also handles the fractional part of the number (but not scientific notation). The fractional part is added to *pn in the same fashion as the integer part:

```
    *pn = 10.0 * *pn + c - '0';
```

Later, *pn is divided by the variable power to adjust the number due to the presence of the fractional part. For each digit collected after the decimal point, the variable power is multiplied by 10. For example, if 0 digits follow the decimal point power equals 1, if 1 digit follows the decimal point power equals 10, and if 3 digits follow the decimal point power equals 1000.

After all digits in the fractional part are recorded, the final number is computed. The final number is multiplied by sign and divided by the variable power:

```
    *pn *= sign / power;
```

As in getint, either EOF is returned or the ASCII value of the character following the number is returned. The type is also an int.

Exercise 5-2:   (page 102 K&R)

Write a pointer version of the function strcat which we showed in Chapter 2: strcat(s, t) copies the string t to the end of s.

```
strcat(s, t)        /* concatenate t to end of s; pointer version */
char *s, *t;
{
    while (*s)
        s++;
    while (*s++ = *t++)
        ;
}
```

Initially, s and t point to the beginning of character strings.

The first while loop increments the pointer s until it finds the end of string marker ('\0'). The statement

```
while (*s)
```

is true as long as the terminating character is not found (*s != '\0').

The second while loop appends the string t to the string s:

```
while (*s++ = *t++)
    ;
```

The above statement assigns what s points to equal to what t points to (*s = *t), increments both pointers (s++, t++), and continues as long as t does not point to the end of string marker (*t != '\0').

Exercise 5-3:   (page 102 K&R)

Write a macro for strcpy.

```
#define strcpy(s, t)   { char *__ps = s, *__pt = t; \
                          while (*__ps++ = *__pt++)  \
                              ;                       \
                       }
```

The macro for strcpy works properly only if the arguments are not __ps or __pt. The behavior of the macro is similar to the routine strcpy (page 101 K&R).

The long definition is continued by placing a \ at the end of the line to be continued (page 86 K&R).

Exercise 5-4:   (page 102 K&R)

Rewrite appropriate programs from earlier chapters and exercises with pointers instead of array indexing. Good possibilities include getline (Chapters 1 and 4), atoi, itoa, and their variants (Chapters 2, 3, and 4), reverse (Chapter 3), and index and getop (Chapter 4).

```
#include  <stdio.h>

getline(s, lim)                    /* get line into s, return length */
char *s;
int lim;
{
    int c;
    char *t = s;

    while (--lim > 0 && (c=getchar()) != EOF && c != '\n')
        *s++ = c;
    if (c == '\n')
        *s++ = c;
    *s = '\0';
    return(s - t);
}
```

The character array s is replaced by a pointer to a character, *s. The variable i, which was the index to the character array s, is not needed. Indexing through the string is performed by incrementing the pointer s.

The statement

```
s[i++] = c;
```

is equivalent to

```
*s++ = c;
```

When s is passed to getline, it points to the first element in the string. *t, which is also a character pointer, is assigned to point to this first element:

```
char *t = s;
```

After a line is fetched, s points to the terminating character ('\0'). t still points to the first character in the line, so the length of the line is s - t.

```
atoi(s)                     /* convert s to integer; pointer version */
char *s;
{
    int n, sign;

    for ( ; *s == ' ' || *s == '\n' || *s == '\t'; s++)
        ;                                       /* skip white space */
    sign = 1;
    if (*s == '+' || *s == '-')                 /* sign of number   */
        sign = (*s++ == '+') ? 1 : -1;
    for (n = 0; *s >= '0' && *s <= '9'; s++)
        n = 10 * n + *s - '0';                  /* value of number  */
    return(sign * n);
}
```

s[i] is equivalent to *s. s[i++] is equivalent to *s++.

```
itoa(n, s)        /* convert n to characters in s; pointer version */
char *s;
int n;
{
    int sign;
    char *t = s;      /* save s (pointer to beginning of string) */

    if ((sign = n) < 0)                        /* record sign      */
        n = -n;
    do {                          /* generate digits in reverse order */
        *s++ = n % 10 + '0';                   /* get next digit   */
    } while ((n /= 10) > 0);                   /* delete it        */
    if (sign < 0)
        *s++ = '-';
    *s = '\0';
    reverse(t);
}
```

The character pointer *t, is initialized to point to the first element in the string:

```
char *t = s;
```

The statement

```
*s++ = n % 10 + '0';
```

is equivalent to

```
s[i++] = n % 10 + '0';
```

The pointer passed to the routine reverse is t, which still points to the first element in the character string. s is not passed since it points to the end of the string (the null terminating character '\0').

```
#include  <stdio.h>

reverse(s)              /* reverse string s in place; pointer version */
char *s;
{
    char *t;
    int c;

    for (t = s + (strlen(s)-1); s < t; s++, t--) {
        c = *s;
        *s = *t;
        *t = c;
    }
}
```

The character array s is replaced by a pointer to a character, *s. The variables i and j, which indexed the array s, are not needed.

Initially, s points to the first element of the string. The character pointer *t initially points to the last element of the string (excluding the terminating '\0'):

```
t = s + (strlen(s)-1)
```

*s is equivalent to s[i] and *t is equivalent to s[j].   The test in the for loop

    s < t

is equivalent to the test

    i < j

s++ has the same effect as incrementing the index i (i++) and t-- has the same effect as decrementing the index j (j--).

```
index(s, t)      /* return index of t in s, -1 if none; ptr vers. */
char *s, *t;
{
    char *b = s;                        /* beginning of string s */
    char *p, *r;

    for (; *s != '\0'; s++) {
        for (p=s, r=t; *r != '\0' && *p == *r; p++, r++)
            ;
        if (*r == '\0')
            return(s - b);
    }
    return(-1);
}
```

s[i] is replaced by *s, s[j] is replaced by *p, and t[k] is replaced by *r. *b is a character pointer that always points to the first element of the string s (s[0]). p = s is equivalent to j = i. r = t is equivalent to k = 0.

When the if statement is true

    if (*r == '\0')

a match exists and the index of t in the string s is returned:

    return(s - b);

```
double atof(s)     /* convert string s to double; pointer version */
char *s;
{
     double val, power;
     int sign;

     for ( ; *s == ' ' || *s == '\n' || *s == '\t'; s++)
          ;                              /* skip white space */
     sign = 1;
     if (*s == '+' || *s == '-')                /* sign of number   */
          sign = (*s++ == '+') ? 1 : -1;
     for (val = 0; *s >= '0' && *s <= '9'; s++)
          val = 10 * val + *s - '0';
     if (*s == '.')
          s++;
     for (power = 1; *s >= '0' && *s <= '9'; s++) {
          val = 10 * val + *s - '0';
          power *= 10;
     }
     return(sign * val / power);
}
```

s[i++] is equivalent to *s++.

```
#include   <stdio.h>
#define    NUMBER    '0'       /* signal that number found   */
#define    TOOBIG    '9'       /* signal that string is too big */

getop(s, lim)    /* get next operator or operand; pointer version */
char *s;
int lim;
{
     char *sl = s + lim;
     int c;

     while ((c = getch()) == ' ' || c == '\t' || c == '\n')
          ;
     if (c != '.' && (c < '0' || c > '9'))
          return(c);
```

```
        *s = c;
        for (s++; (c = getchar()) >= '0' && c <= '9'; s++)
            if (s < sl)
                *s = c;
        if (c == '.') {                        /* collect fraction */
            if (s < sl)
                *s = c;
            for (s++; (c=getchar()) >= '0' && c <= '9'; s++)
                if (s < sl)
                    *s = c;
        }
        if (s < sl) {                          /* number is ok     */
            ungetch(c);
            *s = '\0';
            return(NUMBER);
        } else {                 /*it's too big; skip rest of line */
            while (c != '\n' && c != EOF)
                c = getchar();
            *(sl-1) = '\0';
            return(TOOBIG);
        }
    }
}
```

The if statement, which compares two indexes of the array s,

```
    if (i < lim)
```

is replaced by

```
    if (s < sl)
```

This statement compares two addresses. Since s and sl both point to the same array, the test determines whether s points to an earlier member of the array than sl.

Exercise 5-5:   (page 109 K&R)

Rewrite `readlines` to create lines in an array supplied by main, rather than calling `alloc` to maintain storage. How much faster is the program?

```
#define   MAXLEN    100      /* maximum length of line        */
#define   MAXSTOR   1000     /* size of available storage space */

readlines(lineptr, linestor, maxlines)      /* read input lines */
char *lineptr[];                            /* for sorting      */
char linestor[];
int maxlines;
{
    int len, nlines;
    char line[MAXLEN];
    char *p = linestor;
    char *linestop = linestor + MAXSTOR;

    nlines = 0;
    while ((len = getline(line, MAXLEN)) > 0)
        if (nlines >= maxlines)
            return(-1);
        else if (p + len > linestop)
            return(-1);
        else {
            line[len-1] = '\0';
            strcpy(p, line);
            lineptr[nlines++] = p;
            p += len;
        }
    return(nlines);
}
```

The main routine supplies the array `linestor`, which stores the lines obtained by `readlines`. The character pointer *p is initialized to point to the first element of `linestor`:

```
char *p = linestor;
```

The original routine readlines (page 107 K&R) uses the routine alloc (page 97 K&R):

```
else if ((p = alloc(len)) == NULL)
```

In this version, line is stored in linestor starting at position p. The statement

```
else if (p + len > linestop)
```

ensures that there is available storage in linestor.

Rewriting readlines makes the program slightly faster.

Exercise 5-6:   (page 110 K&R)

Rewrite the routines day_of_year and month_day with pointers instead of indexing.

```
static int a[13] = {
    0, 31, 28, 31, 30, 31, 30, 31, 31, 30, 31, 30, 31
};
static int b[13] = {
    0, 31, 29, 31, 30, 31, 30, 31, 31, 30, 31, 30, 31
};

static int *day_tab[2] = {a, b};

day_of_year(year, month, day)                 /* set day of year  */
int year, month, day;                         /* from month & day */
{
    int leap, *p;

    leap = year%4 == 0 && year%100 != 0 || year%400 == 0;

    p = *(day_tab + leap);
    while (--month)
        day += *++p;
    return(day);
}

month_day(year, yearday, pmonth, pday)        /* set month, day   */
int year, yearday, *pmonth, *pday;            /* from day of year */
{
    int leap, *p;

    leap = year%4 == 0 && year%100 != 0 || year%400 == 0;

    p = *(day_tab + leap);
    while (yearday > *++p)
        yearday -= *p;
    *pmonth = p - *(day_tab + leap);
    *pday = yearday;
}
```

The original two-dimensional integer array day_tab is broken up into 2 arrays of 13 elements each (a, b). *day_tab is an array of pointers. The first element of *day_tab (*day_tab[0]) points to a[0], and the second element of *day_tab (*day_tab[1]) points to b[0].

Initially, the pointer p either points to a[0] (leap equals 0), or b[0] (leap equals 1):

```
p = *(day_tab + leap);
```

The for loop in the original day_of_year routine

```
for (i = 1; i < month; i++)
    day += day_tab[leap][i];
```

is equivalent to the statements

```
p = *(day_tab + leap);
while (--month)
    day += *++p;
```

in the revised day_of_year routine.

In the original month_day routine

```
for (i = 1; yearday > day_tab[leap][i]; i++)
    yearday -= day_tab[leap][i];
```

is equivalent to the statements

```
p = *(day_tab + leap);
while (yearday > *++p)
    yearday -= *p;
```

in the revised month_day routine.

*p is an element in either a or b. *++p first increments the pointer and then accesses the element.

Since no indexing is used, *pmonth is computed as

```
*pmonth = p - *(day_tab + leap);
```

Exercise 5-7:   (page 114 K&R)

Write the program add which evaluates a reverse Polish expression
from the command line. For example,

    add   2 3 4 + *

evaluates   2 x (3+4).

```
#include  <stdio.h>
#define   MAXOP    20    /* max size of operand, operator      */
#define   NUMBER   '0'   /* signal that number found           */
#define   UNKNOWN  '8'   /* signal that unknown operand/operator */
#define   TOOBIG   '9'   /* signal that string is too big       */

main(argc, argv)                  /* reverse Polish desk calculator */
int argc;                         /* command line version            */
char *argv[];
{
    int type;
    char s[MAXOP];
    double op2, atof(), pop(), push();

    while (--argc)
        switch (type = gettype(s, MAXOP, *++argv)) {
        case NUMBER:
            push(atof(s));
            break;
        case '+':
            push(pop() + pop());
            break;
        case '*':
            push(pop() * pop());
            break;
        case '-':
            op2 = pop();
            push(pop() - op2);
            break;
```

```
        case '/':
            op2 = pop();
            if (op2 != 0.0)
                push(pop() / op2);
            else
                printf("zero divisor popped\n");
            break;
        case '=':
            printf("\t%f\n", push(pop()));
            break;
        case 'c':
            clear();
            break;
        case TOOBIG:
            printf("%.20s ... is too long\n", s);
            argc = 1;
            break;
        case UNKNOWN:
        default:
            printf("%.20s ...  unknown operand/operator\n", s);
            argc = 1;
            break;
        }
}

gettype(s, lim, t)     /* determine type of command line argument */
char *s, *t;
int lim;
{
    char *sl = s + lim;

    if (*t != '.' && (*t < '0' || *t > '9'))
        if (*++t) {                            /* unknown operator  */
            *s++ = *(t-1);
            *s++ = *t;
            *s = '\0';
            return(UNKNOWN);
        } else
            return((int)*(t-1));           /* operator          */
    *s++ = *t;                                 /* integer part      */
    while (*++t >= '0' && *t <= '9')
        if (s < sl)
            *s++ = *t;
```

```
        if (*t == '.') {                       /* fractional part    */
            if (s < sl)
                *s++ = *t;
            while (*++t >= '0' && *t <= '9')
                if (s < sl)
                    *s++ = *t;
        }
        if (*t) {                              /* unknown operand    */
            *s++ = *t;
            *s = '\0';
            return(UNKNOWN);
        }

        if (s < sl) {                          /* number is ok       */
            *s = '\0';
            return(NUMBER);
        } else {                               /* number is too big */
            *(sl-1) = '\0';
            return(TOOBIG);
        }
    }
}
```

This solution is based on the reverse Polish desk calculator on page 74 K&R. It uses the routines push, pop and clear (page 75 K&R).

Each operator/operand read in from the command line must be separated by at least one blank space. The routine gettype determines whether the argument is of a known type. If it is a number or one of the operators (+, *, -, /, =, c) then the appropriate value is returned. If it is something else, then either UNKNOWN or the incorrect value is returned.

The routine gettype is broken up into five parts.

The first if statement

```
    if (*t != '.' && (*t < '0' || *t > '9'))
```

is true if the first element of the argument is not a digit and not a decimal point. The statement

```
    if (*++t)
```

is false only if the argument consists of one character and the terminating '\0'. The value of this character is returned. If the statement is false, then an unknown operator has been found.

If the argument is a number, the next group of statements,

```
*s++ = *t;
while (*++t >= '0' && *t <= '9')
      if (s < sl)
          *s++ = *t;
```

reads the argument in and stores it in *s, as long as there is enough storage space available (s < sl).

Next, the decimal point and the fractional part of the number is read in. This part is skipped if a decimal point does not exist (*t != '.').

If there is something following the fractional part besides '\0' or if there is something following the integer part besides a decimal point or '\0', then the operand is of an unknown type; UNKNOWN is returned.

Finally, if there is enough storage space to store the number, NUMBER is returned and if there has not been enough storage then TOOBIG is returned.

If an error should occur while reading in the arguments, argc is set to 1. The while loop in the main routine

```
while (--argc)
```

becomes false and the program ends.

Exercise 5-8:   (page 114 K&R)

Modify the programs entab and detab (written as exercises in Chapter 1) to accept a list of tab stops as arguments. Use the normal tab settings if there are no arguments.

```
#include   <stdio.h>
#define    MAXLINE   100       /* maximum line size      */
#define    TABINC    8         /* default: tab increment size */
#define    YES       1
#define    NO        0

main(argc, argv)   /* entab: replace strings of blanks with tabs */
int argc;          /*          and blanks; command line version   */
char *argv[];
{
     int tab[MAXLINE+1];

     settab(argc, argv, tab);      /* initialize tab stops    */
     entab(tab);                   /* replace strings of blanks */
                                   /* with tabs and blanks      */
}

settab(argc, argv, tab)                    /* initialize tab stops */
int argc;
char *argv[];
int tab[];
{
     int i, pos;

     if (argc <= 1)                      /* default tab stops    */
         for (i = 1; i <= MAXLINE; i++)
             if (i % TABINC == 1)
                 tab[i] = YES;
             else
                 tab[i] = NO;
     else {                             /* provided tab stops    */
         for (i = 1; i <= MAXLINE; i++)
             tab[i] = NO;                /* turn off all tab stops */
         while (--argc) {                /* walk through arg list */
             pos = atoi(*++argv);
```

```
                    if (pos > 0 && pos <= MAXLINE)
                        tab[pos] = YES;      /* turn on selected ones  */
              }
          }
    }

    entab(tab)       /* replace strings of blanks with tabs and blanks */
    int tab[];
    {
        int c, pos;
        int nb = 0;                               /* # of blanks needed */
        int nt = 0;                               /* # of tabs   needed */

        for (pos = 1; (c=getchar()) != EOF; pos++)
            if (c == ' ')
                if (tabpos(pos+1, tab) == NO)
                    ++nb;                         /* insert blank */
                else {
                    nb = 0;           /* replace blanks with a tab */
                    ++nt;
                }
            else {
                while (nt) {                      /* output        */
                    putchar('\t');
                    --nt;
                }
                if (c != '\t')
                    while (nb > 0) {
                        putchar(' ');
                        --nb;
                    }
                else
                    nb = 0;
                putchar(c);
                if (c == '\n')
                    pos = 0;
                else if (c == '\t')
                    while (tabpos(pos+1, tab) != YES)
                        ++pos;
            }
    }
```

```
tabpos(pos, tab)              /* determine if position is a tab stop */
int pos;
int tab[];
{
    if (pos > MAXLINE)
        return(YES);
    else
        return(tab[pos]);
}
```

The framework to this solution is the entab program in Kernighan & Plauger, *Software Tools* (Addison-Wesley, 1976).

Each element in the array tab corresponds to a position within the line, i.e. tab[1] corresponds to the first position within the line (pos equals 1). If the position is a tab stop, then the corresponding element tab[i] equals YES; otherwise tab[i] equals NO.

The tab stops are initialized in the routine settab. If there are no arguments (argc equals 1), then a tab stop is found when the statement

```
if (i % TABINC == 1)
```

is true. If there are arguments, then the element in tab corresponding to each tab stop read from the command line is set equal to YES.

Strings of blanks are replaced by blanks and tabs in the routine entab. This routine is similar to Exercise 1-20.

The routine tabpos determines if the position is a tab stop or if the position is greater than maximum number of characters in a line (MAXLINE). If it is greater than MAXLINE then YES is returned; otherwise tab[pos] is returned.

```
#include  <stdio.h>
#define   MAXLINE  100       /* maximum line size          */
#define   TABINC   8         /* default: tab increment size */
#define   YES      1
#define   NO       0
```

```
main(argc, argv)                /* detab:  replace tab with blanks */
int argc;                       /*         command line version    */
char *argv[];
{
    int tab[MAXLINE+1];

    settab(argc, argv, tab);        /* initialize tab stops   */
    detab(tab);                     /* replace tab with blanks */
}

detab(tab)                              /* replace tab with blanks */
int tab[];
{
    int c, pos = 1;

    while ((c = getchar()) != EOF)
        if (c == '\t') {                            /* tab      */
            do
                putchar(' ');
            while (tabpos(++pos, tab) != YES);
        } else if (c == '\n') {                     /* newline */
            putchar(c);
            pos = 1;
        } else {                                    /* other   */
            putchar(c);
            ++pos;
        }
}
```

The framework to this solution is the detab program in Kernighan & Plauger, *Software Tools* (Addison-Wesley, 1976).

The routines tabpos and settab are the same as found in the first part of this exercise.

Tabs are replaced by blanks in the routine detab. This routine is similar to Exercise 1-19. If a tab is found then blanks are inserted as long as tabpos(++pos, tab) is not equal to YES:

```
do
    putchar(' ');
while (tabpos(++pos, tab) != YES);
```

Exercise 5-9: (page 114 K&R)

Extend entab and detab to accept the shorthand

    entab *m* +*n*

to mean tab stops every *n* columns, starting at column *m*. Choose
convenient (for the user) default behavior.

```
#include  <stdio.h>
#define   MAXLINE   100      /* maximum line size        */
#define   TABINC    8        /* default: tab increment size */
#define   YES       1
#define   NO        0

main(argc, argv)    /* entab: replace strings of blanks with tabs */
int argc;           /*    and blanks; command line version (m +n) */
char *argv[];
{
     int tab[MAXLINE+1];

     esettab(argc, argv, tab);    /* initialize tab stops     */
     entab(tab);                  /* replace strings of blanks */
                                  /* with tabs and blanks     */
}

esettab(argc, argv, tab)                  /* initialize tab stops */
int argc;                                 /* extended version     */
char *argv[];
int tab[];
{
     int i, inc, pos;

     if (argc <= 1)                       /* default tab stops */
          for (i = 1; i <= MAXLINE; i++)
               if (i % TABINC == 1)
                    tab[i] = YES;
               else
                    tab[i] = NO;
```

```
    else if (argc == 3 && *argv[2] == '+') {              /* m +n */
        pos = atoi(*++argv);
        inc = atoi(*++argv);
        for (i = 1; i <= MAXLINE; i++)
            if (i == pos) {
                tab[i] = YES;
                pos += inc;
            } else
                tab[i] = NO;
    } else {                                  /* provided tab stops    */
        for (i = 1; i <= MAXLINE; i++)
            tab[i] = NO;              /* turn off all tab stops */
        while (--argc) {             /* walk through arg list  */
            pos = atoi(*++argv);
            if (pos > 0 && pos <= MAXLINE)
                tab[pos] = YES;    /* turn on selected ones  */
        }
    }
}
```

The framework to this solution is the entab program in Kernighan & Plauger, *Software Tools* (Addison-Wesley, 1976).

This solution is similar to the entab program in Exercise 5-8. The only modification made is that the routine settab is replaced by esettab (extended settab).

esettab accepts the shorthand notation *m +n*. The statements

```
pos = atoi(*++argv);
inc = atoi(*++argv);
```

sets pos equal to the first tab stop and sets inc equal to the increment size. Therefore, the tab stops begin at pos and are every inc positions.

```
#include  <stdio.h>
#define   MAXLINE   100          /* maximum line size       */
#define   TABINC    8            /* default: tab increment size */
#define   YES       1
#define   NO        0

main(argc, argv)               /* detab:  replace tab with blanks */
int argc;                      /*     command line version (m +n) */
char *argv[];
{
    int tab[MAXLINE+1];

    esettab(argc, argv, tab);      /* initialize tab stops    */
    detab(tab);                    /* replace tab with blanks */
}
```

The framework to this solution is the detab program in Kernighan & Plauger, *Software Tools* (Addison-Wesley, 1976).

This solution is similar to the detab program in Exercise 5-8 and uses the routine esettab from the first part of this exercise.

Exercise 5-10: (page 114 K&R)

Write the program tail, which prints the last *n* lines of its input. By default, *n* is 10, let us say, but it can be changed by an optional argument, so that

```
tail -n
```

prints the last *n* lines. The program should behave rationally no matter how unreasonable the input or the value of *n*. Write the program so it makes the best use of available storage: lines should be stored as in sort, not in a two-dimensional array of fixed size.

```
#include   <stdio.h>
#define    DEFLINES  10        /* default # of lines to print   */
#define    LINES     100       /* max # of lines to print       */
#define    MAXLEN    100       /* max length of an input line   */

main(argc, argv)     /* tail: print last n lines of the input   */
int argc;
char *argv[];
{
    int first, i, last, len, n, nlines;
    char *alloc(), *p;
    char line[MAXLEN];              /* current input line        */
    char *lineptr[LINES];           /* pointers to lines read    */

    if (argc == 1)                  /* no argument present       */
        n = DEFLINES;               /* use default # of lines    */
    else if (argc == 2)
        if ((*++argv)[0] == '-')
            n = atoi(argv[0]+1);
        else
            error("usage:  tail [-n]");
    else
        error("usage:  tail [-n]");

    if (n < 1 || n > LINES)         /* unreasonable value for n? */
        n = LINES;
    for (i = 0; i < LINES; i++)
        lineptr[i] = NULL;
    last = 0;                       /* index of last line read   */
```

```
        nlines = 0;                    /* number of lines read       */

        while ((len = getline(line, MAXLEN)) > 0) {
            if (lineptr[last] == NULL)
                if ((lineptr[last] = alloc(MAXLEN)) == NULL)
                    error("tail: cannot allocate line");
            nlines++;
            strcpy(lineptr[last], line);
            if (++last >= LINES)     /* wrap around ?              */
                last = 0;
        }
        if (n > nlines)                /* req. lines more than rec.? */
            n = nlines;
        first = last - n;
        if (first < 0)                 /* it did wrap around the list*/
            first += LINES;
        for (i = first; n-- > 0; i = (i + 1) % LINES)
            printf("%s", lineptr[i]);
    }

error(s)
char *s;
{
    printf("%s\n", s);
    exit(1);
}
```

The variable argc indicates the number of arguments on the command line.
For

```
    tail
```

argc is 1. For

```
    tail -20
```

argc is 2: program name followed by -20.

The program prints the last n lines of its input. When argc is 1, n is set to
the default value DEFLINES. When argc is 2, the value for n is obtained from
the command line. It is an error for argc to be greater than 2.

The loop

```
while ((len = getline(line, MAXLEN)) > 0)
```

gets a line at a time until `getline` (Exercise 1-14) finds the end of its input. For each line read, a buffer is allocated if one is not available:

```
if (lineptr[last] == NULL)
    if ((lineptr[last] = alloc(MAXLEN)) == NULL)
        error("tail: cannot allocate line");
```

MAXLEN characters are allocated, instead of `len` characters, because the buffer may be reused with an unknown number of characters (up to MAXLEN).

The elements of the array `lineptr` point to characters: the last LINES lines read so far. The index for this array is the variable `last`. It starts at 0 and it is incremented after each line is read:

```
if (++last >= LINES)
    last = 0;
```

When `last` becomes equal to LINES it wraps around and the elements of `lineptr` and their buffers are then reused.

The total number of lines is `nlines`. The last n lines are to be printed, so the number of lines requested cannot exceed the number of lines received:

```
if (n > nlines)
    n = nlines;
```

If the total number of lines exceeded LINES, the index `last` wrapped around and the starting index has to be adjusted:

```
if (first < 0)
    first += LINES;
```

The last n lines are then printed:

```
for (i = first; n-- > 0; i = (i + 1) % LINES)
    printf("%s", lineptr[i]);
```

Since i starts with the value of first and goes for n elements it may wrap around. The modulus (remainder) operator maintains i between the values 0 and LINES-1:

```
i = (i + 1) % LINES
```

The standard library function exit (page 154 K&R) terminates the program when an error occurs. exit returns a 1 indicating an error condition.

Exercise 5-11:   (page 117 K&R)

Modify sort to handle a -r flag, which indicates sorting in reverse (decreasing) order. Of course -r must work with -n.

```c
#include <stdio.h>

#define   NUMERIC   1        /* numeric sort                 */
#define   DSORT     2        /* sort in decreasing order     */

#define   LINES     100      /* max number of lines to be sorted */

static char option = 0;      /* bits determine which options set */

main(argc, argv)                        /* sort input lines */
int argc;
char *argv[];
{
    char *s;
    char *lineptr[LINES];       /* pointers to text lines     */
    int nlines;                 /* number of input lines read */
    int strcmp(), numcmp();     /* comparison functions       */
    int swap();                 /* exchange functions         */

    while (--argc  && (*++argv)[0] == '-')
        for (s = argv[0]+1; *s != '\0'; s++)
            switch (*s) {
            case 'n':                          /* numeric sort */
                option |= NUMERIC;
                break;
            case 'r':            /* sort in decreasing order */
                option |= DSORT;
                break;
            default:
                printf("sort: illegal option %c\n", *s);
                argc = 0;
                break;
            }
```

```
        if (argc)
            printf("Usage: sort -nr \n");
        else {
            if ((nlines = readlines(lineptr, LINES)) > 0) {
                if (option & NUMERIC)                    /* numeric */
                    sort(lineptr, nlines, numcmp, swap);
                else                                     /* string  */
                    sort(lineptr, nlines, strcmp, swap);
                writelines(lineptr, nlines, option & DSORT);
            } else
                printf("input too big to sort \n");
        }
}

writelines(lineptr, nlines, order)            /* write output lines */
char *lineptr[];
char order;
int nlines;
{
    int i;

    if (order)                                /* decreasing order */
        for (i = nlines-1; i >= 0; i--)
            printf("%s\n", lineptr[i]);
    else                                      /* increasing order */
        for (i = 0; i < nlines; i++)
            printf("%s\n", lineptr[i]);
}
```

The bits of the static character variable option determines which options are requested.

0th bit	= 0	character string sort	
	= 1	numeric sort	(-n)
1st bit	= 0	sort in increasing order	
	= 1	sort in decreasing order	(-r)

If an option is requested, the bitwise inclusive OR operator (|) is used to set the appropriate bit in the variable option. The statement

```
option |= DSORT;
```

is equivalent to

```
option = option | 2;
```

The decimal number 2 is equivalent to 00000010 in binary. Since

1 OR anything = 1

the above C statement sets the 1st bit in the character variable `option` to 1. (The bits are numbered 0, 1, 2, ... from right to left).

To determine if an option is set, the bitwise AND (&) operator is used.

The expression

```
option & DSORT
```

equals 1 if the -r option is requested and equals 0 if the -r option is not requested.

`writelines` is modified to accept a third argument, `order`. The variable `order` is the result of the expression `option & DSORT`, which determines whether the sorted list is printed in increasing order or decreasing order.

The routines `strcmp`, `numcmp`, `swap`, `sort` and `readlines` are those used in the sort program (page 115 K&R).

Exercise 5-12: (page 117 K&R)

Add the option -f to fold upper and lower case together, so that case
distinctions are not made during sorting: upper and lower case data
are sorted together, so that a and A appear adjacent, not separated by
an entire case of the alphabet.

```
#include <stdio.h>

#define   NUMERIC   1        /* numeric sort                    */
#define   DSORT     2        /* sort in decreasing order        */
#define   FOLDING   4        /* fold upper & lower case together */

#define   LINES     100      /* max number of lines to be sorted */

static char option = 0;      /* bits determine which options set */

main(argc, argv)                         /* sort input lines */
int argc;
char *argv[];
{
    char *s;
    char *lineptr[LINES];    /* pointers to text lines    */
    int nlines;              /* number of input lines read */
    int charcmp(), numcmp(); /* comparison functions      */
    int swap();              /* exchange functions        */

    while (--argc && (*++argv)[0] == '-')
        for (s = argv[0]+1; *s != '\0'; s++)
            switch (*s) {
            case 'f':                        /* folding      */
                option |= FOLDING;
                break;
            case 'n':                        /* numeric sort */
                option |= NUMERIC;
                break;
            case 'r':              /* sort in decreasing order */
                option |= DSORT;
                break;
```

```
                    default:
                        printf("sort: illegal option %c\n", *s);
                        argc = 0;
                        break;
                }

        if (argc)
            printf("Usage: sort -fnr \n");
        else {
            if ((nlines = readlines(lineptr, LINES)) > 0) {
                if (option & NUMERIC)                    /* numeric */
                    sort(lineptr, nlines, numcmp, swap);
                else                                     /* string  */
                    sort(lineptr, nlines, charcmp, swap);
                writelines(lineptr, nlines, option & DSORT);
            } else
                printf("input too big to sort \n");
        }
}

charcmp(s, t)           /* return <0 if s<t, 0 if s==t, >0 if s>t */
char *s, *t;
{
    int fold = (option & FOLDING) ? 1 : 0;              /* 1 = fold */

    for ( ; (fold?lower(*s):*s) == (fold?lower(*t):*t); s++,t++)
        if (*s == '\0')
            return(0);
    return((fold) ? (lower(*s) - lower(*t)) : (*s - *t));
}
```

The framework to this solution is Exercise 5-11.

2nd bit   = 0   no folding
           = 1   folding   (-f)

If the fold option is requested, the second bit in option must be set equal to
1:

```
option | = FOLDING;
```

In binary notation, decimal 4 (FOLDING) is 00000100 (The bits are numbered 0, 1, 2, 3, ... from right to left).

The function charcmp compares strings similar to strcmp (page 101 K&R), but also allows upper and lower case characters to be folded together.

If the fold option is requested, then the two characters compared in the routine charcmp are first converted to lower case. The comparison is made and the pointers are incremented. The for statement handles these three steps:

```
for ( ; (fold?lower(*s):*s) == (fold?lower(*t):*t); s++,t++)
```

Converting each character to lower case, while not changing the contents of storage, has the effect of folding upper and lower case characters together. If the fold option is requested, the value returned is the distance between two lower case characters (lower(*s) - lower(*t)). It should be noted that the same result is obtained if each character is converted to upper case.

The routines numcmp, swap, sort, readlines and writelines are those used in Exercise 5-11.

Exercise 5-13: (page 117 K&R)

Add the -d ("dictionary order") option, which makes comparisons
only on letters, numbers, and blanks. Make sure it works in
conjunction with -f.

```
#include    <stdio.h>
#include    <ctype.h>

#define     NUMERIC    1        /* numeric sort                     */
#define     DSORT      2        /* sort in decreasing order         */
#define     FOLDING    4        /* fold upper & lower case together */
#define     DICTION    8        /* dictionary order                 */

#define     LINES      100      /* max number of lines to be sorted */

static char option = 0;         /* bits determine which options set */

main(argc, argv)                           /* sort input lines */
int argc;
char *argv[];
{
    char *s;
    char *lineptr[LINES];       /* pointers to text lines       */
    int nlines;                 /* number of input lines read   */
    int charcmp(), numcmp();    /* comparison functions         */
    int swap();                 /* exchange functions           */

    while (--argc  && (*++argv)[0] == '-')
        for (s = argv[0]+1; *s != '\0'; s++)
            switch (*s) {
            case 'd':                       /* dictionary order */
                option |= DICTION;
                break;
            case 'f':                       /* folding          */
                option |= FOLDING;
                break;
            case 'n':                       /* numeric sort     */
                option |= NUMERIC;
                break;
```

```
                case 'r':                    /* sort in decreasing order */
                    option | = DSORT;
                    break;
                default:
                    printf("sort: illegal option %c\n", *s);
                    argc = 0;
                    break;
            }
        if (argc)
            printf("Usage: sort -dfnr \n");
        else {
            if ((nlines = readlines(lineptr, LINES)) > 0) {
                if (option & NUMERIC)                   /* numeric */
                    sort(lineptr, nlines, numcmp, swap);
                else                                    /* string  */
                    sort(lineptr, nlines, charcmp, swap);
                writelines(lineptr, nlines, option & DSORT);
            } else
                printf("input too big to sort \n");
        }
    }


charcmp(s, t)              /* return <0 if s<t, 0 if s==t, >0 if s>t */
char *s, *t;
{
    char a, b;
    int fold = (option & FOLDING) ? 1 : 0;
    int dict = (option & DICTION) ? 1 : 0;
```

```
    do {
        if (dict) {                         /* dictionary order */
            while (!isalnum(*s) && *s != ' ' && *s != '\0')
                s++;
            while (!isalnum(*t) && *t != ' ' && *t != '\0')
                t++;
        }
        a = (fold) ? lower(*s++) : *s++;
        b = (fold) ? lower(*t++) : *t++;
        if (a == b && a == '\0')
            return(0);
    } while (a == b);

    return(a - b);
}
```

The framework to this solution is Exercises 5-11 and 5-12.

3rd bit = 0   no dictionary order
       = 1   dictionary order   (-d)

If the dictionary option is requested, the third bit in option must be set to 1.

    option |= DICTION;

In binary notation, decimal 8 (DICTION) is 00001000 (The bits are numbered 0, 1, 2, 3, ... from right to left).

The charcmp routine (Exercise 5-12) is modified to handle both the fold option and the dictionary option.

The variable dict is assigned the value 1 if the dictionary option is requested. The variable fold is assigned the value 1 if the fold option is requested.

The character variables, a and b, temporarily hold the value pointed to by s and the value pointed to by t, respectively. This reduces the number of times the function lower has to be called.

If the dictionary option is requested, then the while loop

```
    while (!isalnum(*s) && *s != ' ' && *s != '\0')
        s++;
```

examines each character in the string s and skips over those characters which are not letters, numbers, and blanks. The macro isalnum is defined in ctype.h, which is part of the standard C library. This header file defines machine-independent tests for determining the properties of characters. isalnum tests for alphabetic characters (a-z, A-Z) and digits (0-9). If *s is an alphabetic character or a digit then isalnum(*s) is nonzero; otherwise isalnum(*s) is zero.

The next while loop

```
while (!isalnum(*t) && *t != ' ' && *t != '\0')
    t++;
```

examines each character in the string t and skips over those characters which are not letters, numbers, and blanks.

When a letter, number, or blank is found in s and a letter, number or blank is found in t, the two characters are compared.

Due to the dictionary option, the do-while loop is needed since the comparison (a == b) cannot be made until the letters are checked.

The routines numcmp, swap, sort, readlines and writelines are those used in Exercise 5-11.

Exercise 5-14:   (page 117 K&R)

Add a field-handling capability, so sorting may be done on fields
within lines, each field according to an independent set of options.
(The index for this book was sorted with -df for the index category
and -n for the page numbers.)

```
#include   <stdio.h>
#include   <ctype.h>

#define   NUMERIC   1        /* numeric sort                         */
#define   DSORT     2        /* sort in decreasing order             */
#define   FOLDING   4        /* fold upper & lower case together     */
#define   DICTION   8        /* dictionary order                     */

#define   LINES     1000     /* max number of lines to be sorted     */

static char option = 0;      /* bits determine which options set     */

main(argc, argv)                              /* sort input lines    */
int argc;
char *argv[];
{
    char *lineptr[LINES];    /* pointers to text lines       */
    int i;
    int nlines;              /* number of input lines read   */
    int pos1 = 0;            /* field beginning with pos1     */
    int pos2 = 0;            /* ending just before pos2       */
    int charpcmp(), numpcmp();   /* comparison functions      */
    int swap();              /* exchange functions           */

    readargs(argc, argv, &pos1, &pos2);
    if ((nlines = readlines(lineptr, LINES)) > 0) {
        if (option & NUMERIC)                          /* numeric */
            sort(lineptr, nlines, numpcmp, swap, pos1, pos2);
        else                                           /* string */
            sort(lineptr, nlines, charpcmp, swap, pos1, pos2);
        writelines(lineptr, nlines, option & DSORT);
    } else
        printf("input too big to sort \n");
}
```

```
readargs(argc, argv, pos1, pos2)                    /* read arguments */
int argc;
char *argv[];
int *pos1, *pos2;
{
    char *s, t;

    while (--argc)
        if ((t=(*++argv)[0]) != '-' && t != '+')
            error("Usage: sort -dfnr [+pos1][-pos2]");
        else if (t == '-' &&
                (*(argv[0]+1) < '0' || *(argv[0]+1) > '9'))
            for (s = argv[0]+1; *s != '\0'; s++)
                switch (*s) {
                case 'd':                    /* dictionary order */
                    option |= DICTION;
                    break;
                case 'f':                    /* folding          */
                    option |= FOLDING;
                    break;
                case 'n':                    /* numeric sort     */
                    option |= NUMERIC;
                    break;
                case 'r':          /* sort in decreasing order */
                    option |= DSORT;
                    break;
                default:
                    printf("sort: illegal option %c\n", *s);
                    error("Usage: sort -dfnr [+pos1][-pos2]");
                    break;
                }
        else if (t == '+') {                            /* pos1 */
            *pos1 = atoi(argv[0]+1);
            if (--argc)
                if ((*++argv)[0] == '-') {              /* pos2 */
                    *pos2 = atoi(argv[0]+1);
                    if (--argc)
                        error(
                         "Usage: sort -dfnr [+pos1][-pos2]");
                    else if (*pos1 >= *pos2 && *pos2 != 0)
                        error("readargs: pos1 >= pos2");
                    else
                        break;
```

```
                    } else
                            error("Usage: sort -dfnr [+pos1][-pos2]");
                else
                    break;
            } else {
                *pos2 = atoi(argv[0]+1);                    /* pos2 */
                if (--argc)
                    error("Usage: sort -dfnr [+pos1][-pos2]");
                else if (*pos1 >= *pos2 && *pos2 != 0)
                    error("readargs: pos1 >= pos2");
                else
                    break;
            }
    }
}

sort(v, n, comp, exch, pos1, pos2) /* sort strings v[0] ... v[n] */
char *v[];
int n, pos1, pos2;
int (*comp)(), (*exch)();
{
    int gap, i, j;

    for (gap = n/2; gap > 0; gap /= 2)
        for (i = gap; i < n; i++)
            for (j = i-gap; j >= 0; j -= gap) {
                if ((*comp)(v[j], v[j+gap], pos1, pos2) <= 0)
                    break;
                (*exch)(&v[j], &v[j+gap]);
            }
}

charpcmp(s, t, pos1, pos2)      /* <0 if s<t, 0 if s==t, >0 if s>t */
char s[], t[];
int pos1, pos2;
{
    char a, b;
    int i, j;
    int dict = (option & DICTION) ? 1 : 0;
    int fold = (option & FOLDING) ? 1 : 0;
```

```
        i = j = pos1;
        if (pos2 == 0)                       /* ending pos not specified ? */
            if((pos2 = strlen(s)) > strlen(t))
                pos2 = strlen(t);    /* take length of short string*/
        do {
            if (dict) {                             /* dictionary order */
                while (i < pos2 && !isalnum(s[i]) &&
                        s[i] != ' ' && s[i] != '\0')
                    i++;
                while (j < pos2 && !isalnum(t[j]) &&
                        s[j] != ' ' && s[j] != '\0')
                    j++;
            }
            if (i < pos2 && j < pos2) {
                a = (fold) ? lower(s[i++]) : s[i++];
                b = (fold) ? lower(t[j++]) : t[j++];
                if (a == b && a == '\0')
                    return(0);
            }
        } while (a == b && i < pos2 && j < pos2);

        return(a - b);
}

#define    MAXSTR    100

numpcmp(s1, s2, pos1, pos2)    /* compare s1 and s2 numerically    */
char *s1, *s2;
int pos1, pos2;
{
        double atof(), v1, v2;
        char str[MAXSTR];

        substr(s1, pos1, pos2, str, MAXSTR);
        v1 = atof(str);
        substr(s2, pos1, pos2, str, MAXSTR);
        v2 = atof(str);
```

```
        if (v1 < v2)
            return(-1);
        else if (v1 > v2)
            return(1);
        else
            return(0);
}

substr(s, pos1, pos2, str, maxlen)      /* get substring from s  */
char s[], str[];
int pos1, pos2, maxlen;
{
    int i, j, len;

    len = strlen(s);
    if (pos2 == 0 )                     /* ending pos not specified?  */
        pos2 = len;
    if (len < pos1 || len < pos2)
        error("substr: string too short");
    if (pos2 - pos1 > maxlen)
        error("substr: string too long");
    for (j = 0, i = pos1; i < pos2; i++, j++)
        str[j] = s[i];
    str[j] = '\0';
}

error(s)                                /* print error message and exit */
char *s;
{
    printf("%s\n", s);
    exit(1);
}
```

The framework to this solution is Exercises 5-11, 5-12 and 5-13.

The syntax of the sort command is

```
sort -dfnr [+pos1] [-pos2]
```

If sorting on fields within lines is desired, then the sort begins at pos1 and ends just before pos2. Otherwise pos1 and pos2 are equal to 0 and the entire line is sorted.

The routine readargs reads the command line arguments and sets the appropriate variables. An argument is read for each loop of the while statement.

The first if statement

```
if ((t=(*++argv)[0]) != '-' && t != '+')
```

is false if the arguments are specified incorrectly (not preceded by a minus sign (-) or a plus sign (+)).

The first else-if statement

```
else if (t == '-' &&
        (*(argv[0]+1) < '0' || *(argv[0]+1) > '9'))
```

is true if the argument is a minus sign followed by a non-digit. The switch statement processes these arguments the same way as in Exercises 5-11, 5-12 and 5-13.

The next else-if statement

```
else if (t == '+')
```

is true only if the argument specified is the optional +pos1. The value of pos1 is calculated and tests are made to determine if -pos2 is on the command line:

```
if (--argc)
    if ((*++argv)[0] == '-')
```

If -pos2 is found, then the value of pos2 is calculated. Error messages are produced if pos1 is greater than or equal to pos2 (only if pos2 is specified) or if something other than -pos2 follows +pos1 or if something follows -pos2. The function error prints the error message and invokes the function exit (page 154 K&R) which terminates the program.

The final else statement processes -pos2 when +pos1 is not on the command line.

The sort routine is modified: pos1 and pos2 are passed to sort and then to the comparison routine. charpcmp is a modified version of charcmp which handles fields. numpcmp compares numbers like numcmp but requires a new routine substr since atof does not take origin and length as arguments. It is safer to invent a new routine substr rather to change the interface of a highly used function like atof. The sub-strings are sorted, however the entire line gets exchanged, if necessary.

The routines swap, readlines and writelines are those used in Exercise 5-11.

Exercise 6-1: (page 128 K&R)

Make this modification to getword and measure the change in speed of the program.

```
#define   DIG   '0'                          /* digit */
#define   LET   'a'                          /* letter */

int type[129] = {
      -1,   0,   1,   2,   3,   4,   5,   6,   7,   8,   9,  10,
      11,  12,  13,  14,  15,  16,  17,  18,  19,  20,  21,  22,
      23,  24,  25,  26,  27,  28,  29,  30,  31, ' ', '!', '"',
     '#', '$', '%', '&','\'', '(', ')', '*', '+', ',', '-', '.',
     '/', DIG, DIG, DIG, DIG, DIG, DIG, DIG, DIG, DIG, DIG, ':',
     ';', '<', '=', '>', '?', '@', LET, LET, LET, LET, LET, LET,
     LET, LET, LET, LET, LET, LET, LET, LET, LET, LET, LET, LET,
     LET, LET, LET, LET, LET, LET, LET, LET, '[','\\', ']', '^',
     '_', '` ', LET, LET, LET, LET, LET, LET, LET, LET, LET, LET,
     LET, LET, LET, LET, LET, LET, LET, LET, LET, LET, LET, LET,
     LET, LET, LET, LET, '{', '|', '}', '~ ', 127
     };

getword(w, lim)                          /* get next word from input */
char *w;
int lim;
{
     int c, t;

     if (type[(c = *w++ = getch()) + 1] != LET) {
         *w = '\0';
         return(c);
     }
```

```
    while (--lim > 0) {
        t = type[(c = *w++ = getch()) + 1];
        if (t != LET && t != DIG) {
            ungetch(c);
            break;
        }
    }
    *(w-1) = '\0';
    return(LET);
}
```

The function type is replaced by an integer array type of size 129. The array is only useful for the ASCII character set when EOF is −1.

The index of the array type is the ASCII value of a character plus 1. The addition of 1 is meant to handle the EOF (−1). Therefore, if an EOF is found, then type[-1+1] = type[0] is accessed and if a 'A' is found (ASCII value 65) then type[65+1] = type[66] is accessed.

This modification slightly increases the speed of the program.

Exercise 6-2:   (page 128 K&R)

Write a version of type which is independent of character set.

```
#define    DIGIT      '0'
#define    LETTER     'a'

type(c)     /* return type of character (independent of char set) */
int c;
{
    switch (c) {
    case 'A': case 'B': case 'C': case 'D': case 'E': case 'F':
    case 'G': case 'H': case 'I': case 'J': case 'K': case 'L':
    case 'M': case 'N': case 'O': case 'P': case 'Q': case 'R':
    case 'S': case 'T': case 'U': case 'V': case 'W': case 'X':
    case 'Y': case 'Z':
    case 'a': case 'b': case 'c': case 'd': case 'e': case 'f':
    case 'g': case 'h': case 'i': case 'j': case 'k': case 'l':
    case 'm': case 'n': case 'o': case 'p': case 'q': case 'r':
    case 's': case 't': case 'u': case 'v': case 'w': case 'x':
    case 'y': case 'z':
        return(LETTER);
    case '0': case '1': case '2': case '3': case '4':
    case '5': case '6': case '7': case '8': case '9':
        return(DIGIT);
    default:
        return(c);
    }
}
```

The solution is to have a case statement for each upper case letter, each lower case letter, and each digit. Since there is no guarantee that the alphabet is contiguous and the number set is contiguous in every character set, ranges such as the ones used in type (page 127 K&R):

```
(c >= 'a' && c <= 'z' || c >= 'A' && c <= 'Z')
```

and

```
(c >= '0' && c <= '9')
```

cannot be used.

Exercise 6-3:   (page 128 K&R)

Write a version of the keyword-counting program which does not count occurrences contained within quoted strings.

```
#include  <stdio.h>
#define   DIGIT    '0'
#define   LETTER   'a'
#define   MAXWORD  20

#define   NKEYS    (sizeof(keytab)/sizeof(struct key))

main()                                    /* count C keywords */
{
    int n, t;
    char word[MAXWORD];

    while ((t = getword(word, MAXWORD)) != EOF)
        if (t == LETTER)
            if ((n = binary(word, keytab, NKEYS)) >= 0)
                keytab[n].keycount++;

    for (n = 0; n < NKEYS; n++)
        if (keytab[n].keycount > 0)
            printf("%4d %s\n",
                keytab[n].keycount, keytab[n].keyword);
}

getword(w, lim)                           /* get next word from input */
char *w;
int lim;
{
    int c, t;
```

```
if ((t = type(c = *w++ = getch()))) != LETTER) {
    if (t == '"')                    /* ignore quoted strings */
        while ((c = getch()) != '"' && c != EOF)
            if (c == '\\')
                getch();
    *w = '\0';
    return(c);
}
while (--lim > 0) {
    t = type(c = *w++ = getch());
    if (t != LETTER && t != DIGIT) {
        ungetch(c);
        break;
    }
}
*(w-1) = '\0';
return(LETTER);
}
```

This solution assumes that all double quotes are balanced. Otherwise, the solution is invalid.

The only modification made is in the routine getword. The main routine, the routine binary, the routine type and the structure keytab are unchanged. If type returns a double quote, then the while loop is executed until another double quote or an EOF is fetched. If an EOF is found, then a terminating double quote is missing:

```
if (t == '"')
    while ((c = getch()) != '"' && c != EOF)
        if (c == '\\')
            getch();
```

If a backslash is fetched when in the while loop, the character following the backslash is skipped. Within double quotes, the double quote following a backslash, \", is not interpreted as the closing double quote. For example,

```
printf("\"hello\"");
```

would produce the output

```
"hello"
```

Exercise 6-4:   (page 134 K&R)

Write a program which reads a C program and prints in alphabetical order each group of variable names which are identical in the first 7 characters, but different somewhere thereafter. (Make sure that 7 is a parameter).

```
#include  <stdio.h>
#define   DIGIT    '0'
#define   LETTER   'a'
#define   MAXWORD  20
#define   YES      1
#define   NO       0

struct tnode {                    /* the basic node       */
    char *word;                   /* points to the text */
    int match;                    /* match found          */
    struct tnode *left;           /* left child           */
    struct tnode *right;          /* right child          */
};

main(argc, argv)      /* prints in alphabetic order each group of  */
int argc;             /* variable names that are identical in the  */
char *argv[];         /* num characters (7 = default)              */
{
    struct tnode *root, *treex();
    char word[MAXWORD];
    int found;            /* = YES (1) if a match is found    */
    int num;              /* number of chars to be distinct in */
    int t;

    num = (--argc && (*++argv)[0] == '-') ? atoi(argv[0]+1) : 7;
    root = NULL;
    found = NO;
    while ((t = getword(word, MAXWORD)) != EOF) {
        if (t == LETTER && strlen(word) >= num)
            root = treex(root, word, num, &found);
        found = NO;
    }
    treeprint(root);
}
```

```
struct tnode *treex(p, w, num, found) /* install w at or below p */
struct tnode *p;
char *w;
int num;
int *found;
{
    struct tnode *talloc();
    char *strsave();
    int cond;

    if (p == NULL) {                    /* a new word has arrived */
        p = talloc();                   /* make a new node        */
        p->word = strsave(w);
        p->match = *found;
        p->left = p->right = NULL;
    } else if ((cond = compare(w, p, num, found)) < 0)
        p->left = treex(p->left, w, num, found);
    else if (cond > 0)
        p->right = treex(p->right, w, num, found);
    return(p);
}

compare(s, p, num, found)    /* compare words and update p->match */
char *s;
struct tnode *p;
int num;
int *found;
{
    char *t = p->word;
    int i;

    for (i = 0; *s == *t; i++, s++, t++)
        if (*s == '\0')
            return(0);
    if (i >= num) {        /* identical in first num characters ? */
        *found = YES;
        p->match = YES;
    }
    return(*s - *t);
}
```

```
treexprint(p)        /* print each element of tree if p->match = 1 */
struct tnode *p;
{
    if (p != NULL) {
        treexprint(p->left);
        if (p->match)
            printf("%s\n", p->word);
        treexprint(p->right);
    }
}

type(c)                      /* return type of ASCII character */
int c;
{
    if (c >= 'a' && c <= 'z' || c >= 'A' && c <= 'Z' || c == '_')
        return(LETTER);
    else if (c >= '0' && c <= '9')
        return(DIGIT);
    else
        return(c);
}
```

The variable num is the number of characters for the variable name to be identical in. If it is not specified on the command line, then it is set to 7:

```
num = (--argc && (*++argv)[0] == '-') ? atoi(argv[0]+1) : 7;
```

The variable found is a boolean. found equals YES (1) if the word is identical in num characters to a word in the tree and equals NO (0) if no match is found. found is initialized to NO.

The word is placed in the tree if getword (page 127 K&R) returns LETTER and the length of the word is greater than or equal to num. The routine treex, which is a modification of tree (page 132 K&R), installs the word in the tree. treex, rather than calling strcmp, calls the routine compare.

The routine compare compares the word being placed in the tree to a word already in the tree. If a match is found in the first num characters, then *found and the match member (p->match) corresponding to the word in the tree are set equal to YES (1):

```
if (i >= num) {
    *found = YES;
    p->match = YES;
}
```

The routine `treexprint` prints the words in the tree that are identical to at least one other word.

```
if (p->match)
    printf("%s\n", p->word);
```

To handle the underscore as a letter, the routine `type` (page 127 K&R), which is used by `getword`, is modified. In the C Programming Language, the underscore (_) is considered a letter (page 33 K&R).

Exercise 6-5:   (page 134 K&R)

Write a basic cross-referencer: a program which prints a list of all
words in a document, and, for each word, a list of the line numbers
on which it occurs.

```
#include  <stdio.h>
#define   LETTER    'a'
#define   MAXWORD   20

struct linklist {               /* linked list of line numbers */
    int lnum;
    struct linklist *ptr;
};

struct tnode {                          /* the basic node     */
    char *word;                         /* points to the text */
    struct linklist *lines;             /* line numbers       */
    struct tnode *left;                 /* left child         */
    struct tnode *right;                /* right child        */
};

main()                          /* basic cross-referencer */
{
    struct tnode *root, *treex();
    char word[MAXWORD];
    int t, linenum;

    linenum = 1;
    root = NULL;
    while ((t = getword(word, MAXWORD)) != EOF)
        if (t == LETTER)
            root = treex(root, word, linenum);
        else if (t == '\n')
            linenum++;
    treexprint(root);
}
```

```
struct tnode *treex(p, w, linenum)    /* install w at or below p */
struct tnode *p;
char *w;
int linenum;
{
    struct tnode *talloc();
    struct linklist *lalloc();
    char *strsave();
    int cond;

    if (p == NULL) {                       /* a new word has arrived */
        p = talloc();
        p->word = strsave(w);
        p->lines = lalloc();
        p->lines->lnum = linenum;
        p->lines->ptr = NULL;
        p->left = p->right = NULL;
    } else if ((cond = strcmp(w, p->word)) == 0)
        addln(p, linenum);
    else if (cond < 0)
        p->left = treex(p->left, w, linenum);
    else
        p->right = treex(p->right, w, linenum);
    return(p);
}

addln(p, linenum)          /* add a line number to the linked list */
struct tnode *p;
int linenum;
{
    struct linklist *temp, *lalloc();

    temp = p->lines;
    while (temp->ptr != NULL && temp->lnum != linenum)
        temp = temp->ptr;
    if (temp->lnum != linenum) {
        temp->ptr = lalloc();
        temp->ptr->lnum = linenum;
        temp->ptr->ptr = NULL;
    }
}
```

```
treexprint(p)                                        /* print tree */
struct tnode *p;
{
      struct linklist *temp;

      if (p != NULL) {
          treexprint(p->left);
          printf("%10s:  ", p->word);
          for (temp = p->lines; temp != NULL; temp = temp->ptr)
              printf("%4d ", temp->lnum);
          printf("\n");
          treexprint(p->right);
      }
}

struct linklist *lalloc()
{
      char *alloc();

      return((struct linklist *) alloc(sizeof(struct linklist)));
}

struct tnode *talloc()
{
      char *alloc();

      return((struct tnode *) alloc(sizeof(struct tnode)));
}
```

The tree contains one node per distinct word. Each node contains

    a pointer to the text of the word (*word)
    a pointer to a linked list of line numbers (*lines)
    a pointer to the left child node (*left)
    a pointer to the right child node (*right)

The linked list of line numbers is a structure of type linklist. Each element of the list contains a line number and a pointer to the next element in the linked list. When there are no more elements in the list, the pointer is NULL.

The routine treex is a modified version of tree (page 132 K&R). treex installs the word in the tree and the line number on which it occurs in the

corresponding linked list. If a new word has arrived, then the first element in
the linked list gets assigned the line number:

```
p->lines->lnum = linenum;
```

If a word already in the tree has arrived,

```
((cond = strcmp(w, p->word)) == 0)
```

then the routine addln adds the line number to the linked list.

addln traverses through the linked list looking for an occurrence of the same
line number or NULL:

```
while (temp->ptr != NULL && temp->lnum != linenum)
    temp = temp->ptr;
```

If the line number is not found, the routine adds a new element at the end of
the linked list:

```
if (temp->lnum != linenum) {
    temp->ptr = lalloc();
    temp->ptr->lnum = linenum;
    temp->ptr->ptr = NULL;
}
```

If the line number is found, then the line number is not added again to the
linked list.

treexprint is a modified version of treeprint (page 133 K&R). treexprint
prints the tree in alphabetical order. For each word in the tree, this routine
prints the word and all line numbers on which the word occurred.

Exercise 6-6:   (page 134 K&R)

Write a program which prints the distinct words in its input sorted into decreasing order of frequency of occurrence. Precede each word by its count.

```
#include    <stdio.h>
#define     LETTER      'a'
#define     MAXWORD     20
#define     NDISTINCT 1000

struct tnode {                          /* the basic node           */
    char *word;                         /* points to the text       */
    int count;                          /* number of occurrences */
    struct tnode *left;                 /* left child               */
    struct tnode *right;                /* right child              */
};

static struct tnode *list[NDISTINCT];
static int n = 0;                       /* number of distinct words */

main()                      /* print distinct words with frequency */
{
    struct tnode *root, *tree();
    char word[MAXWORD];
    int i, t;

    root = NULL;
    while ((t = getword(word, MAXWORD)) != EOF)
        if (t == LETTER)
            root = tree(root, word);
    treestore(root);
    sort1();
    for (i = 0; i < n; i++)
        printf("%2d:%20s\n", list[i]->count, list[i]->word);
}
```

```
treestore(p)                /* stores the tree in the array list[] */
struct tnode *p;
{
    if (p != NULL) {
        treestore(p->left);
        if (n < NDISTINCT)
            list[n++] = p;
        treestore(p->right);
    }
}

sort1()                                          /* sort the list */
{
    int gap, i, j;
    struct tnode *temp;

    for (gap = n/2; gap > 0; gap /= 2)
        for (i = gap; i < n; i++)
            for (j = i-gap; j >= 0; j -=gap) {
                if ((list[j]->count) <= (list[j+gap]->count))
                    break;
                temp = list[j];
                list[j] = list[j+gap];
                list[j+gap] = temp;
            }
}
```

NDISTINCT is the maximum number of distinct words allowed. The structure tnode is the one used on page 131 K&R. *list is an array of pointers, each pointer pointing to a structure of type tnode. The variable n is a counter that contains the number of distinct words. Both n and *list are declared static prior to the routines so they are known to the main routine, treestore, sort1, and no other files.

Each word is fetched from input and placed in the tree. The routine treestore, then stores each pointer to tnode in the array list. list[n] points to the same structure as p does. This assignment occurs as long as there are less than NDISTINCT words.

The routine sort1 is a modification of the routine shell (page 58 K&R). sort1 sorts the array *list according to list[j]->count.

Exercise 6-7:   (page 136 K&R)

Write a routine which will remove a name and definition from the table maintained by lookup and install.

```
remove(s)                    /* remove name s and def from hashtab  */
char *s;
{
     struct nlist *prev, *np;
     int h;

     prev = NULL;
     h = hash(s);              /* hash value of string s            */
     for (np = hashtab[h]; np != NULL; np = np->next) {
          if (strcmp(s, np->name) == 0)
               break;
          prev = np;           /* remember previous entry           */
     }
     if (np != NULL) {         /* found name                        */
          if (prev == NULL)    /* first in the hash list ?          */
               hashtab[h] = np->next;
          else                 /* somewhere else in the hash list */
               prev->next = np->next;
          free(np->name);
          free(np->def);
          free(np);            /* free allocated structure          */
     }
}
```

The routine remove looks for the string s in the table. When it finds the string it exits the loop:

```
if (strcmp(s, np->name) == 0)
     break;
```

If the string s is not found, the for loop terminates when the pointer np becomes NULL.

If np is not NULL there is a name and a definition to be removed from the table. An entry in hashtab points to the beginning of a linked list. np points to the entry to be removed and prev points to an entry just preceding np.

When prev is NULL then np is the first entry in the linked list starting at hashtab[h]:

```
if (prev == NULL)
    hashtab[h] = np->next;
else
    prev->next = np->next;
```

After removing the np entry, the space allocated for the name, the definition, and for the structure itself are freed (free page 177 K&R):

```
free(np->name);
free(np->def);
free(np);
```

Exercise 6-8:   (page 136 K&R)

Implement a simple version of the #define processor suitable for use
with C programs, based on the routines of this section. You may also
find getch and ungetch helpful.

```
#include  <stdio.h>

#define   DIGIT    '0'
#define   LETTER   'a'
#define   MAXWORD  100

struct nlist {                          /* basic table entry        */
      char *name;
      char *def;
      struct nlist *next;               /* next entry in the chain */
};

main()                      /* simple version of #define processor */
{
      int typ;
      char w[MAXWORD];
      struct nlist *p, *lookup();

      while ((typ = getword(w, MAXWORD)) != EOF)
            if (strcmp(w, "#") == 0)       /* beginning of directive */
                  getdef();
            else if (typ != LETTER)        /* can not be defined     */
                  printf("%s", w);
            else if ((p = lookup(w)) == NULL)
                  printf("%s", w);              /* not defined       */
            else
                  ungets(p->def);          /* push definition        */
}
```

```
getdef()                                /* get definition and install it */
{
    int i, typ;
    char def[MAXWORD], dir[MAXWORD], name[MAXWORD];

    skipblanks();
    if ((typ = getword(dir, MAXWORD)) != LETTER)
        error(dir[0], "getdef: expecting a directive after #");
    else if (strcmp(dir, "define") == 0) {
        skipblanks();
        if ((typ = getword(name, MAXWORD)) != LETTER)
            error(name[0], "getdef: non-alpha - name expected");
        else {
            skipblanks();
            for (i = 0; i < MAXWORD-1; i++)
                if ((def[i] = getch()) == EOF ||
                        def[i] == '\n')
                    break;              /* end of definition  */
            def[i] = '\0';
            if (i <= 0)                     /* no definition ?    */
                error('\n', "getdef: incomplete define");
            else
                install(name, def);    /* install definition */
        }
    } else if (strcmp(dir, "undef") == 0) {
        skipblanks();
        if ((typ = getword(name, MAXWORD)) != LETTER)
            error(name[0], "getdef: non-alpha in undef");
        else
            remove(name);
    } else
        error(dir[0], "getdef: expecting a directive after #");
}

error(c, s)          /* print error message and skip rest of line */
int c;
char *s;
{
    printf("error: %s\n", s);
    while (c != EOF && c != '\n')
        c = getch();
}
```

```
skipblanks()                              /* skip blanks and tabs */
{
     int c;

     while ((c = getch()) == ' ' || c == '\t')
          ;
     ungetch(c);                          /* push back non-blank character */
}
```

The main program contains the body of this simple processor. Directives
(define, undef) are expected to follow a # and the function getdef resolves
that. If the word received from getword is not alphanumeric then it could
not have been defined. Alphanumeric words are searched for possible defini-
tions. When a definition exists the function ungets (Exercise 4-4) pushes it
back in reverse order onto the input stream.

The function getdef handles the directives:

```
#define    name       definition
#undef     name
```

The name is expected to be alphanumeric.

In a define, the loop

```
for (i = 0; i < MAXWORD-1; i++)
     if ((def[i] = getch()) == EOF ||
          def[i] == '\n')
          break;
```

gathers the definition until it finds the end of the line (or end of file). If a
definition exists it is installed in the table using the install function (page
136 K&R).

An undef directive causes a name to be removed from the table (Exercise
6-7).

Exercise 7-1: (page 147 K&R)

Write a program which will print arbitrary input in a sensible way.
As a minimum, it should print non-graphic characters in octal or hex
(according to local custom), and fold long lines.

```
#include  <stdio.h>
#include  <ctype.h>

#define   MAXLINE  100      /* max number of chars in one line */
#define   OCTLEN   6        /* length of an octal value        */

main()                 /* print arbitrary input in a sensible way  */
{
    int c, pos;

    pos = 0;                          /* position in the line      */
    while ((c = getchar()) != EOF)
        if (iscntrl(c) || c == ' ') {
                                      /* non-graphic or blank      */
            pos = inc(pos, OCTLEN);
            printf(" \\%03o ", c);
            if (c == '\n') {    /* newline character ?       */
                putchar('\n');
                pos = 0;
            }
        } else {                      /* graphic character         */
            pos = inc(pos, 1);
            putchar(c);
        }
}
```

```
inc(pos, n)              /* increment position counter for output      */
int pos, n;
{
    if (pos + n < MAXLINE)
        return(pos+n);
    else {
        putchar('\n');
        return(n);
    }
}
```

The length of an output line is MAXLINE. The macro iscntrl is defined in
ctype.h, which is part of the standard C library. iscntrl finds the non-
graphic characters: the delete character (octal 0177) and ordinary control
characters (less than octal 040). Blanks are also considered non-graphic characters. Non-graphic characters are printed in octal (preceded by a blank and a
\ and followed by a blank) using OCTLEN positions. A newline character resets
pos:

```
if (c == '\n') {
    putchar('\n');
    pos = 0;
}
```

The function inc returns the last position used and folds a line if there is not
n places available for output.

Exercise 7-2:   (page 151 K&R)

Rewrite the desk calculator of Chapter 4 using scanf and/or sscanf
to do the input and number conversion.

```
#include   <stdio.h>
#include   <ctype.h>
#define    MAXSTR    80        /* maximum string size            */
#define    MAXUSE    MAXSTR-2  /* usable string: str+' '+'\0'    */
#define    NUMBER    '0'       /* signal that number found       */
#define    TOOBIG    '9'       /* signal that string is too big  */

getop(s, lim)                  /* get next operator or operand   */
char s[];
int lim;
{
    int i = 1;
    int c = ' ';               /* start with a blank character   */
    char iostr[MAXSTR];
    static char lastchar[] = " ";

    sscanf(lastchar, "%1s", &c);
    if (c != ' ')              /* a character had been saved     */
        lastchar[0] = ' ';     /* clear last character saved     */
    else
        if (scanf("%1s", &c) == EOF)
            c = EOF;           /* found end of input             */
    if (c != '.' && !isdigit(c))
        return(c);             /* operator or EOF                */
    sprintf(iostr, "%c", c);   /* save character in iostr        */
    if (c != '.')              /* gather digits before fraction  */
        while (scanf("%c", &c) != 0 && i < MAXUSE)
            if (isdigit(c))
                sprintf(&iostr[i++], "%c", c);
            else
                break;     /* not a digit                    */
```

```
        if (c == '.') {              /* gather digits after the decimal */
            if (i < MAXUSE)
                sprintf(&iostr[i++], "%c", c);
            while (scanf("%c", &c) != 0 && i < MAXUSE)
                if (isdigit(c))
                    sprintf(&iostr[i++], "%c", c);
                else
                    break;      /* not a digit                  */
        }
        iostr[i++] = ' ';            /* string delimiter for sscanf  */
        iostr[i]   = '\0';           /* end of string                */
        if (strlen(iostr)-1 < lim) { /* number is OK                 */
            sscanf(iostr, "%s", s);
            lastchar[0] = c;         /* went one char too far        */
            return(NUMBER);
        } else {                     /* number is too big            */
            iostr[lim-1] = ' ';      /* shorten current string       */
            sscanf(iostr, "%s", s);
            while (scanf("%c", &c) != EOF && c != '\n');
                ;                    /* skip the rest of the line    */
            return(TOOBIG);          /* overflow signal              */
        }
    }
}
```

The function getop (page 78 K&R) is the only routine modified.

One thing to remember between calls to getop is the character following a
number. lastchar is a one element static array that remembers the last character read (sscanf expects a string).

The control

```
    "%1s"
```

for scanf or sscanf looks for a non-white character.

The call

```
    sscanf(lastchar, "%1s", &c);
```

reads a character only if the last character seen in the previous call was non-white. Otherwise, c is not changed (it is still a blank character.) If the last character was a white character, the statement

```
if (scanf("%1s", &c) == EOF)
```

reads the first non-white character from input.

The first non-white character determines whether the current input is an operator or an operand. If the character is neither a decimal point nor a digit, it is an operator or EOF. If it is an operand the first character is pushed onto the string iostr:

```
sprintf(iostr, "%c", c);
```

That character was the first character of an operand. It could be a decimal point or a digit. If it was not a decimal point getop reads one character at a time until it finds a non-digit (this is the part in front of the decimal point, if present). If getop finds a decimal point (at the beginning of the operand or after the integer part of a number) it reads the digits following the decimal point.

White characters delimit strings for scanf and sscanf.

The statement

```
iostr[i++] = ' ';
```

marks the end of the string of digits in iostr for sscanf, and the statement

```
iostr[i]    = '\0';
```

marks the end of the string for strlen.

If there was no overflow (the length of iostr is less than lim), getop returns NUMBER, returns the string of digits copied from iostr, and remembers the last character read. If there was an overflow, getop returns TOOBIG, returns lim-1 characters copied from iostr, and discards the rest of the input line.

The macro isdigit is defined in ctype.h. It returns a nonzero for true when the argument is the ASCII representation for a digit (0-9), otherwise it returns 0 for false.

Exercise 7-3:   (page 156 K&R)

Write a program to compare two files, printing the first line and character position where they differ.

```
#include  <stdio.h>
#define   MAXLINE   100

main(argc, argv)           /* compare two files - main program   */
int argc;
char *argv[];
{
    FILE *fp1, *fp2, *fopen();

    if (argc != 3) {      /* incorrect number of arguments ?      */
        fprintf(stderr, "comp: need two file names\n");
        exit(1);
    } else {
        if ((fp1 = fopen(*++argv, "r")) == NULL) {
            fprintf(stderr, "comp: can't open %s\n", *argv);
            exit(1);
        } else if ((fp2 = fopen(*++argv, "r")) == NULL) {
            fprintf(stderr, "comp: can't open %s\n", *argv);
            exit(1);
        } else {          /* found and opened files to be compared*/
            filecomp(fp1, fp2);
            fclose(fp1);
            fclose(fp2);
            exit(0);
        }
    }
}

filecomp(fp1, fp2)         /* compare two files - a line at a time */
FILE *fp1, *fp2;
{
    char line1[MAXLINE], line2[MAXLINE];
    char *lp1, *lp2;
    int pos;
```

```
        do {
             lp1 = fgets(line1, MAXLINE, fp1);
             lp2 = fgets(line2, MAXLINE, fp2);
             if (lp1 == line1 && lp2 == line2) {
                  if ((pos = linecomp(line1, line2)) >= 0) {
                       printf("first difference at position %d", pos);
                       printf(" in line\n%s\n", line1);
                       lp1 = lp2 = NULL;
                  }
             } else if (lp1 != line1 && lp2 == line2) {
                  printf("first difference at position 0");
                  printf(" in line\n%s\n", line2);
             } else if (lp1 == line1 && lp2 != line2) {
                  printf("first difference at position 0");
                  printf(" in line\n%s\n", line1);
             }
        } while (lp1 == line1 && lp2 == line2);
   }

   linecomp(s, t)              /* return -1 if s == t, pos otherwise   */
   char *s, *t;
   {
        int pos;

        for (pos = 0; *s == *t; s++, t++, pos++)
             if (*s == '\0')
                  return(-1);        /* the strings do match      */
        return(pos);                 /* position where they differ */
   }
```

The number of arguments should be three: program name followed by two
file names. The files are opened and filecomp compares them a line at a
time.

filecomp reads a line from each file. The function fgets returns a pointer to
the line read or NULL on end of file. If lp1 and lp2 point to their respective
lines, neither file has ended and the two lines are compared. When the lines
do not match, then filecomp prints the position where they differ and the
current line from the first file.

If lp1 or lp2 do not point to their respective lines, one of the files has ended
(EOF) and a line has no match at position 0.

If both lp1 and lp2 do not point to their respective lines, both files have ended (EOF) — they did not differ.

The function linecomp is similar to strcmp (page 102 K&R). linecomp returns −1 if the lines match. Otherwise, it returns the first position where the lines do not match.

Exercise 7-4: (page 156 K&R)

Modify the pattern finding program of Chapter 5 to take its input
from a set of named files or, if no files are named as arguments,
from the standard input. Should the file name be printed when a
matching line is found?

```c
#include  <stdio.h>
#define   MAXLINE   100

main(argc, argv)           /* find pattern from first argument    */
int argc;
char *argv[];
{
    char line[MAXLINE], pattern[MAXLINE], *s;
    long lineno = 0;
    int except = 0, number = 0;
    FILE *fopen(), *fp;

    while (--argc > 0 && (*++argv)[0] == '-')
        for (s = argv[0]+1; *s != '\0'; s++)
            switch (*s) {
            case 'x':
                except = 1;
                break;
            case 'n':
                number = 1;
                break;
            default:
                printf("find: illegal option %c\n", *s);
                argc = 0;
                break;
            }
    if (argc >= 1)
        copy(*argv, pattern);
    else {
        printf("Usage: find [-x] [-n] pattern [file . . .]\n");
        exit(1);
    }
```

```
      if (argc == 1)              /* read standard input       */
          fpat(stdin, "\0", pattern, except, number);
      else
          while (--argc > 0)  /* get a named file              */
              if ((fp = fopen(*++argv, "r")) == NULL) {
                  fprintf(stderr, "find: can't open %s\n",
                          *argv);
                  exit(1);
              } else {        /* named file has been opened    */
                  fpat(fp, *argv, pattern, except, number);
                  fclose(fp);
              }
}

fpat(fp, fname, pattern, except, number)      /* find pattern    */
FILE *fp;
char *fname, *pattern;
int except, number;
{
    char line[MAXLINE];
    long lineno = 0;

    while (fgets(line, MAXLINE, fp) != NULL) {
        ++lineno;
        if ((index(line, pattern) >= 0) != except) {
            if (*fname != '\0')              /* have a file name */
                printf("%s - ", fname);
            if (number)                      /* print line number*/
                printf("%ld: ", lineno);
            printf("%s\n", line);
        }
    }
}
```

The main program processes the optional arguments as in Chapter 5 (page
113 K&R). After that, it expects at least one more argument — the pattern.
If file names do not follow the pattern, it uses the standard input. Otherwise,
it opens a named file. In either case, it invokes fpat.

Most of the function fpat is similar to the code in the original main program.
It reads a line at a time until fgets (page 155 K&R) returns NULL. It looks
for the specified pattern in each line. The possibilities are:

(index(line, pattern) >= 0)	!=	except	result
0 (did not find pattern)	!=	0 (not specified)	false
1 (found pattern)	!=	0 (not specified)	true
0 (did not find pattern)	!=	1 (specified)	true
1 (found pattern)	!=	1 (specified)	false

When the result of that expression is true, fpat prints the file name (unless it is the standard input), the line number if it was asked for, and the line itself.

Exercise 7-5:   (page 156 K&R)

Write a program to print a set of files, starting each new one on a
new page, with a title and a running page count for each file.

```
#include   <stdio.h>
#define    MAXBOT     3           /* maximum # lines at bottom page  */
#define    MAXHDR     5           /* maximum # lines at head of page */
#define    MAXLINE    100         /* maximum size of one line        */
#define    MAXPAGE    66          /* maximum # lines in one page      */

main(argc, argv)     /* print files - each new one on a new page  */
int argc;
char *argv[];
{
    FILE *fopen(), *fp;

    if (argc == 1)       /* no arguments; copy standard input    */
        fileprint(stdin, "");
    else
        while (--argc > 0)
            if ((fp = fopen(*++argv, "r")) == NULL) {
                fprintf(stderr,
                        "print: can't open %s\n", *argv);
                exit(1);
            } else {
                fileprint(fp, *argv);
                fclose(fp);
            }
    exit(0);
}
```

```
fileprint(fp, fname)                /* print file fname          */
FILE *fp;
char *fname;
{
    long lineno = 1;
    long pageno = 1;
    long heading();
    char line[MAXLINE];

    fprintf(stdout, "\f");   /* start a file on a new page      */
    while (fgets(line, MAXLINE, fp) != NULL) {
        if (lineno % MAXPAGE == 1)
            lineno = heading(fname, pageno++);
        fputs(line, stdout);
        ++lineno;
        if (lineno > MAXPAGE - MAXBOT)
            do {
                    fprintf(stdout, "\n");
            } while (++lineno <= MAXPAGE);
    }
}

long heading(fname, pageno)    /* put heading & skip MAXHDR lines */
char *fname;
long pageno;
{
    long ln = 3;

    fprintf(stdout, "\n\n"); /* two blank lines at top of page  */
    fprintf(stdout, "%s    page %d\n", fname, pageno);
    while (ln++ < MAXHDR)
        fprintf(stdout, "\n");
    return(ln);
}
```

The program is similar to cat (page 154 K&R).

The function fileprint takes two arguments: a pointer to an opened file and a pointer to the file name (an empty string when the file is the standard input). fileprint reads and prints lines. The character

   \f

is the form feed. It starts each file on a new page.

The variable lineno counts the number of lines. The page length is MAXPAGE. When the remainder of lineno and MAXPAGE is equal to 1,

```
if (lineno % MAXPAGE == 1)
    lineno = heading(fname, pageno++);
```

fileprint puts a new heading and resets lineno. The function heading prints the file name and page number then puts enough newline characters so that MAXHDR lines are used at the top of the page.

MAXBOT is the number of blank lines at the bottom of the page.

CHAPTER 8:   THE UNIX SYSTEM INTERFACE

Exercise 8-1:   (page 164 K&R)

Rewrite the program cat from Chapter 7 using read, write, open and close instead of their standard library equivalents. Perform experiments to determine the relative speeds of the two versions.

```
#include   <stdio.h>
#define    BUFSIZE    512

main(argc, argv)      /* cat: concatenate files - read / write    */
int argc;
char *argv[];
{
      int fd;

      if (argc == 1)      /* no arguments; copy standard input    */
            filecopy(0);
      else
            while (--argc > 0)
                  if ((fd = open(*++argv, 0)) == -1)
                        error("cat: can't open %s", *argv);
                  else {
                        filecopy(fd);
                        close(fd);
                  }
      exit(0);
}
```

```
filecopy(fd)
int fd;
{
    int n;
    char buf[BUFSIZE];

    while ((n = read(fd, buf, BUFSIZE)) > 0)
        if (write(1, buf, n) != n)
            error("cat: write error", NULL);
}

error(s1, s2)          /* print error message and die          */
char *s1, *s2;
{
    printf(s1, s2);
    printf("\n");
    exit(1);
}
```

The statement

```
if ((fd = open(*++argv, 0)) == -1)
```

opens a file for reading and returns a file descriptor (an integer); it returns a −1 if an error occurs.

The function filecopy reads BUFSIZE characters using the file descriptor fd. read returns a byte count of the characters actually read. While the byte count is greater than 0 there are no errors; a 0 indicates end of file and a −1 indicates an error. The function write writes n bytes, otherwise an error has occurred.

This version is about twice as fast as the original version in Chapter 7 K&R.

Exercise 8-2:   (page 165 K&R)

Clearly, seek can be written in terms of lseek, and vice versa. Write
each in terms of the other.

```
lseek(fd, offset, origin)              /* lseek in terms of seek    */
int fd, origin;
long offset;
{
    seek(fd, (int) (offset / 512), origin + 3);
    seek(fd, (int) (offset % 512), 1);
}
```

lseek in terms of seek:

The value of the long variable offset is converted into the number of
blocks, an integer, so

```
    seek(fd, (int) (offset / 512), origin + 3);
```

determines the correct block. The origin plus the constant 3 converts the possible value 0, 1, or 2 into 3, 4, or 5. The latter values indicate that the
number of blocks is to be multiplied by 512, then interpret the origin as 0, 1,
or 2 respectively.

The next statement,

```
    seek(fd, (int) (offset % 512), 1);
```

finds the correct position within the block, starting at the current position.
(offset % 512) represents a fraction of a block, if any.

```
seek(fd, offset, origin)              /* seek in terms of lseek    */
int fd, offset, origin;
{
    long l;
    int neworigin;

    if ((neworigin = origin % 3) == origin)
        l = (long) offset;                    /* origin: 0, 1, 2  */
    else
        l = (long) (offset * 512);            /* origin: 3, 4, 5  */
    lseek(fd, l, neworigin);
}
```

seek in terms of lseek:

The origin can take a value between 0 and 5 inclusive. When it is between 3 and 5, it indicates that the offset is to be multiplied by the block size and converted to a long integer. When it is between 0 and 2, it indicates that the offset is to be converted to a long integer.

Exercise 8-3:   (page 169 K&R)

Rewrite fopen and _fillbuf with fields instead of explicit bit operations.

```
#define    "nstdio.h"            /* non-standard stdio.h          */
#define    PMODE      0644       /* R/W for owner; R for others   */

FILE *fopen(name, mode)          /* open file, return file ptr    */
register char *name, *mode;
{
    register int fd;
    register FILE  *fp;

    if (*mode != 'r' && *mode != 'w' && *mode != 'a') {
        fprintf(stderr, "illegal mode %s opening %s\n",
                mode, name);
        exit(1);
    }
    for (fp = _iob; fp < _iob + _NFILE; fp++)
        if (fp->_flag.is_read == 0 && fp->_flag.is_write == 0)
            break;              /* found free slot               */
    if (fp >= _iob + _NFILE) /* no free slots                    */
        return(NULL);

    if (*mode == 'w')          /* access file                    */
        fd = creat(name, PMODE);
    else if (*mode == 'a') {
        if ((fd = open(name, 1)) == -1)
            fd = creat(name, PMODE);
        lseek(fd, 0L, 2);
    } else
        fd = open(name, 0);
    if (fd == -1)              /* couldn't access mode            */
        return(NULL);
```

```
        fp->_fd = fd;
        fp->_cnt = 0;
        fp->_base = NULL;
        fp->_flag.is_unbuf = 0;
        fp->_flag.is_buf = 1;
        fp->_flag.is_eof = 0;
        fp->_flag.is_err = 0;
        if (*mode == 'r') {        /* read                    */
            fp->_flag.is_read = 1;
            fp->_flag.is_write = 0;
        } else {                   /* write                   */
            fp->_flag.is_read = 0;
            fp->_flag.is_write = 1;
        }
        return(fp);
}

_fillbuf(fp)                       /* allocate and fill input buffer */
register FILE *fp;
{
        static char smallbuf[_NFILE];     /* for unbuffered I/O    */
        char *calloc();

        if (fp->_flag.is_read == 0 ||
            fp->_flag.is_eof  == 1 ||
            fp->_flag.is_err  == 1 )
            return(EOF);

        while (fp->_base == NULL)          /* find buffer space     */
            if (fp->_flag.is_unbuf)        /* unbuffered            */
                fp->_base = &smallbuf[fp->_fd];
            else if ((fp->_base = calloc(_BUFSIZE, 1)) == NULL)
                fp->_flag.is_unbuf = 1;
            else
                fp->_flag.is_buf = 1;
        fp->_ptr = fp->_base;
        fp->_cnt = read(fp->_fd, fp->_ptr,
                    fp->_flag.is_unbuf ? 1 : _BUFSIZE);
```

```
        if (--fp->_cnt < 0) {
            if (fp->_cnt == -1)
                fp->_flag.is_eof = 1;
            else
                fp->_flag.is_err = 1;
            fp->_cnt = 0;
            return(EOF);
        }
        return(*fp->_ptr++ & 0377);            /* make char positive    */
}
```

A copy of stdio.h is made and called nstdio.h (non-standard stdio.h). The bit field changes apply only to these modified versions of fopen and _fillbuf.

The typedef for struct _iobuf is shown on page 165 K&R. One of the members of _iobuf is

```
int  _flag;
```

The variable _flag is redefined in terms of bit fields:

```
struct _flag_field {
     unsigned is_read  : 1;
     unsigned is_write : 1;
     unsigned is_unbuf : 1;
     unsigned is_buf   : 1;
     unsigned is_eof   : 1;
     unsigned is_err   : 1;
};
```

The structure template _flag_field is then used in _iobuf:

```
typedef struct _iobuf {
     char *_ptr;
     int  _cnt;
     char *_base;
     struct _flag_field _flag;
     int  _fd;
} FILE;
```

With those changes in nstdio.h, the function fopen (page 167 K&R) is modified.

In the statement

```
if ((fp->_flag & (_READ | _WRITE)) == 0)
    break;
```

the values _READ and _WRITE are OR'ed together:

```
(_READ   |   _WRITE)
   01    |   02        octal
   01    |   10        binary
         11            result
```

This means the if statement is true when both lower order bits of _flag are off (neither read nor write). It verifies that an entry in _iob is not being used for read or write.

Bit fields explicitly test for the condition:

```
if (fp->_flag.is_read == 0 && fp->_flag.is_write == 0)
    break;
```

The next modification explicitly sets the bits:

```
fp->_flag.is_unbuf = 0;
fp->_flag.is_buf = 1;
fp->_flag.is_eof = 0;
fp->_flag.is_err = 0;
```

The other modification in the code

```
fp->_flag &= ~(_READ | _WRITE);
```

turns off the read and write flag bits because

```
(_READ   |   _WRITE)
   01    |   02        octal
   01    |   10        binary
         11            result
       ~(11)
     1...100
```

This value bitwise AND fp->_flag turns off the last two bits of _flag (read and write bits). It leaves the other bits as they were.

Next,

```
fp->_flag |= (*mode == 'r') ? _READ : _WRITE;
```

sets _flag according to mode. If it is 'r', it sets _flag to _READ, otherwise it sets _flag to _WRITE.

With bit fields, if the mode is 'r' the bit is_read is set to 1. If not, the is_write bit is set to 1:

```
if (*mode == 'r') {
    fp->_flag.is_read = 1;
    fp->_flag.is_write = 0;
} else {
    fp->_flag.is_read = 0;
    fp->_flag.is_write = 1;
}
```

The function _fillbuf changes similarly.

The function _fillbuf returns an EOF for following situations: the file was not open for reading, an end of file already happened, or an error has already been detected:

```
if ((fp->_flag & _READ) == 0 || (fp->_flag & (_EOF | _ERR)) != 0)
    return(EOF);
```

These bits are tested with bit fields:

```
if (fp->_flag.is_read == 0 ||
    fp->_flag.is_eof  == 1 ||
    fp->_flag.is_err  == 1 )
    return(EOF);
```

Next,

```
if (fp->_flag & _UNBUF)
```

becomes

```
    if (fp->_flag.is_unbuf)
```

and the segment

```
        fp->_flag |= _UNBUF;
    else
        fp->_flag |= _BIGBUF;
```

becomes

```
        fp->_flag.is_unbuf = 1;
    else
        fp->_flag.is_buf = 1;
```

The test part of the conditional expression

```
    fp->_flag & _UNBUF ? 1 : _BUFSIZE
```

changes to

```
    fp->_flag.is_unbuf ? 1 : _BUFSIZE
```

Finally,

```
        fp->_flag |= _EOF;
    else
        fp->_flag |= _ERR;
```

becomes

```
        fp->_flag.is_eof = 1;
    else
        fp->_flag.is_err = 1;
```

The code in this exercise is valid for UNIX version 7. stdio.h has changed in later versions.

Exercise 8-4:   (page 169 K&R)

Design and write the routines _flushbuf and fclose.

```
#include  <stdio.h>

_flushbuf(x, fp)              /* allocate and flush output buffer    */
char x;
register FILE *fp;
{
     static char smallbuf[_NFILE];    /* for unbuffered I/O    */
     char *calloc();
     int nc;                          /* # chars to flush      */

     if ((fp->_flag & _WRITE) == 0 || (fp->_flag & _ERR) != 0)
          return(EOF);
     if (fp->_base == NULL) {         /* no allocated buffer   */
          while (fp->_base == NULL)   /* find buffer space     */
               if (fp->_flag & _UNBUF)  /* unbuffered          */
                    fp->_base = &smallbuf[fp->_fd];
               else if ((fp->_base = calloc(_BUFSIZE, 1)) == NULL)
                    fp->_flag |= _UNBUF;
               else
                    fp->_flag |= _BIGBUF;
     } else {                         /* buffer already exists */
          nc = fp->_ptr - fp->_base;
          if (write(fp->_fd, fp->_base, nc) != nc)
               return(EOF);           /* error: return EOF     */
     }
     fp->_ptr = fp->_base;            /* beginning of buffer   */
     *fp->_ptr++ = x;                 /* save current char     */
     fp->_cnt = ((fp->_flag & _BIGBUF) ? _BUFSIZE : 1) - 1;
     return(x);
}

fclose(fp)                              /* close file            */
register FILE *fp;
{
     int rc;                            /* return code           */
     int nc;                            /* # of chars to flush   */
```

```
        rc = 0;                          /* return 0 for success  */
        if (fp < _iob || fp >= _iob + _NFILE)
                return(EOF);             /* error: invalid pointer*/
        if (fp->_flag & _WRITE)          /* anything to flush ?   */
                if ((nc = fp->_ptr - fp->_base) > 0)
                        if (write(fp->_fd, fp->_base, nc) != nc)
                                rc = EOF;         /* write error          */
        if (fp->_flag & _BIGBUF)         /* free allocated buffer */
                cfree(fp->_base);
        fp->_ptr = NULL;
        fp->_cnt = 0;
        fp->_base = NULL;
        fp->_flag &= ~(_READ | _WRITE);
        return(rc);
}
```

If the file was not open for writing or an error has occurred, _flushbuf returns an EOF:

```
if ((fp->_flag & _WRITE) == 0 || (fp->_flag & _ERR) != 0)
        return(EOF);
```

The first time _flushbuf is called no buffer exists for output and fp->_base is NULL. A buffer is then allocated as in _fillbuf (page 168 K&R). In subsequent calls to _flushbuf the characters saved in the buffer are flushed:

```
nc = fp->_ptr - fp->_base;
if (write(fp->_fd, fp->_base, nc) != nc)
        return(EOF);
```

nc is the number of characters in the buffer. _flushbuf writes nc characters and returns EOF if an error occurred.

The arguments for _flushbuf are a character and a file pointer. A buffer is then allocated or flushed. The next step is to save the character argument in the buffer:

```
*fp->_ptr++ = x;
```

The number of possible characters in the buffer (fp->_cnt) is then one less than the buffer size because of the character just saved.

The function fclose ensures that fp is a file pointer. If it is not, fclose returns EOF:

```
if (fp < _iob || fp >= _iob + _NFILE)
    return(EOF);
```

The return code is 0 if no errors exist.

If the file was open for writing it might be necessary to flush some characters. The variable nc contains the number of buffered characters. If an error occurs in the write statement then the return code is EOF. The buffer space is freed if a big buffer had been allocated:

```
if (fp->_flag & _BIGBUF)
    cfree(fp->_base);
```

The last step resets members of the _iobuf structure so that fopen will not encounter meaningless values in a free slot.

The code in this exercise is valid for UNIX version 7. stdio.h has changed in later versions.

Exercise 8-5: (page 169 K&R)

The standard library provides a function

```
fseek(fp, offset, origin)
```

which is identical to lseek except that fp is a file pointer instead of a file descriptor. Write fseek. Make sure that your fseek coordinates properly with the buffering done for the other functions of the library.

```c
#include  <stdio.h>

fseek(fp, offset, origin)       /* seek with a file pointer      */
register FILE *fp;
long offset;
int origin;
{
    int nc;                     /* number of characters to flush */
    long rc = 0;                /* return code                   */
    long lseek();

    if (fp->_flag & _READ) {
        if (origin == 1)        /* from current position ?       */
            offset -= fp->_cnt; /* remember chars in buffer      */
        rc = lseek(fp->_fd, offset, origin);
        fp->_cnt = 0;           /* no characters buffered        */
    } else if (fp->_flag & _WRITE) {
        if ((nc = fp->_ptr - fp->_base) > 0)
            if (write(fp->_fd, fp->_base, nc) != nc)
                rc = -1;
        if (rc != -1)           /* no errors yet ?               */
            rc = lseek(fp->_fd, offset, origin);
    }
    return(rc == -1 ? -1 : 0);
}
```

The variable rc contains the return code. It is set to −1 when an error occurs.

There are two situations in fseek: the file is open for reading or it is open for writing.

When the file is open for reading and the origin is 1, the offset is counted from the current position (the other cases are: origin 0, the offset is counted from the beginning of the file; origin 2, the offset is counted from the end of the file). To measure the offset from the current position, fseek takes into account the characters already in the buffer:

```
if (origin == 1)
    offset -= fp->_cnt;
```

fseek then invokes lseek and discards the buffered characters:

```
rc = lseek(fp->_fd, offset, origin);
fp->_cnt = 0;
```

When the file is open for writing, fseek first flushes buffered characters, if any:

```
if ((nc = fp->_ptr - fp->_base) > 0)
    if (write(fp->_fd, fp->_base, nc) != nc)
        rc = -1;
```

If no error exists, lseek is called:

```
if (rc != -1)
    rc = lseek(fp->_fd, offset, origin);
```

The function fseek returns 0 for proper seeks.

Exercise 8-6:   (page 177 K&R)

The standard library function calloc(n, size) returns a pointer to n objects of size size, with the storage initialized to zero. Write calloc, using alloc either as a model or a function to be called.

```
#include  <stdio.h>

char *calloc(n, size)     /* allocate n elements, each with "size"*/
unsigned n, size;
{
    unsigned i, nb;
    char *alloc(), *p, *q;

    nb = n * size;
    if ((p = q = alloc(nb)) != NULL)
        for (i = 0; i < nb; i++)
            *p++ = 0;
    return(q);
}
```

The function calloc allocates n objects of size size. The total number of bytes to be allocated is nb:

```
    nb = n * size;
```

alloc returns a pointer to a storage area of nb bytes. The pointers p and q remember the beginning of this allocated storage area. If the allocation was successful, the nb bytes allocated are initialized to 0:

```
    for (i = 0; i < nb; i++)
        *p++ = 0;
```

calloc returns a pointer to the beginning of the allocated and initialized storage area.

Exercise 8-7:   (page 177 K&R)

alloc accepts a size request without checking its plausibility; free
believes that the block it is asked to free contains a valid size field.
Improve these routines to take more pains with error checking.

```
#include  <stdio.h>

#define   MAXBYTES  (unsigned) 10240

static unsigned maxalloc;/* max number of units allocated      */

char *alloc(nbytes)         /* general-purpose storage allocator   */
unsigned nbytes;
{
    HEADER *morecore();
    register HEADER *p, *q;
    register int nunits;

    if (nbytes > MAXBYTES) {        /* not more than MAXBYTES     */
        fprintf(stderr,
                "alloc: can't allocate more than %u bytes\n",
                MAXBYTES);
        return(NULL);
    }
    nunits = 1 + (nbytes + sizeof(HEADER) - 1) / sizeof(HEADER);

    /* . . . */               /* as on page 175 K&R          */

}

#define   NALLOC    128            /* # units to allocate at once*/

static HEADER *morecore(nu)        /* ask system for memory      */
unsigned nu;
{
    char *sbrk();
    register char *cp;
    register HEADER *up;
    register int rnu;
```

```
        rnu = NALLOC * ((nu + NALLOC - 1) / NALLOC);
        cp = sbrk(rnu * sizeof(HEADER));
        if ((int)cp == -1)              /* no space at all         */
            return(NULL);
        up = (HEADER *)cp;
        up->s.size = rnu;
        maxalloc = (up->s.size > maxalloc) ? up->s.size : maxalloc;
        free((char *)(up+1));
        return(allocp);
    }

free(ap)                    /* put block ap in free list         */
char *ap;
{
    register HEADER *p, *q;

    p = (HEADER *)ap - 1;           /* point to header           */
    if (p->s.size == 0 || p->s.size > maxalloc) {
        fprintf(stderr, "free: can't free %u units\n",
                p->s.size);
        return;
    }
    for (q = allocp; !(p > q && p < q->s.ptr); q = q->s.ptr)

    /* . . . */                     /* as on page 177 K&R         */
}
```

The alloc function checks the number of bytes requested against some arbitrary constant MAXBYTES. Select a value for MAXBYTES that works best for your system.

When morecore allocates a new block the static variable maxalloc remembers the size of the largest block used so far. This way the function free can verify the value of size: it is not 0 and it is not larger than the largest block allocated.

Exercise 8-8:   (page 177 K&R)

Write a routine bfree(p, n) which will free an arbitrary block p of n characters into the free list maintained by alloc and free. By using bfree, a user can add a static or external array to the free list at any time.

```
bfree(p, n)                  /* free an arbitrary block p of n chars */
char *p;
unsigned n;
{
    register HEADER *hp;

    if (n < sizeof(HEADER))
        return(NULL);                /* too small to be useful     */
    hp = (HEADER *) p;
    hp->s.size = n / sizeof(HEADER);
    free((char *)(hp+1));
    return((int)hp->s.size);
}
```

The routine bfree takes two arguments: a pointer p and a number of characters n. It will free the block only if its size is at least sizeof(HEADER), otherwise it returns NULL.

The pointer p is cast to HEADER type and assigned to hp:

```
hp = (HEADER *) p;
```

The size of the block in units of sizeof(HEADER) is:

```
hp->s.size = n / sizeof(HEADER);
```

The last step is to call the function free. Since free accepts a pointer to an area just past the header area, (hp+1) is used. Last, (hp+1) is cast to type (char *).

The routine bfree returns NULL if the block is too small, otherwise it returns the size of the block in sizeof(HEADER) units.

INDEX

TEAR OUT THIS PAGE TO ORDER THESE OTHER HIGH QUALITY C LANGUAGE AND UNIX* SYSTEM TITLES FROM THE WORLD'S PREMIER C/UNIX PUBLISHER— PRENTICE-HALL

Quantity	Title/Author	ISBN	Price	Total $
_____	1. The C Programming Language; Kernighan/Ritchie	013–110163–3	$24.95 paper	_____
_____	2. The C Answer Book; Tondo/ Gimpel	013–109877–2	$17.95 paper	_____
_____	3. The UNIX* Programming Environment; Kernighan/Pike	013–937699–2	$26.95 cloth	_____
_____	4. The C Puzzle Book; Feuer	013–109934–5	$21.95 cloth	_____
_____	5. C: A Reference Manual, 2/E Harbison/Steele	013-109810-1	$28.95 cloth	_____
_____	6. The Design of the UNIX* Operating System; Bach	013–201799–7	$31.95 cloth	_____
_____	7. Advanced UNIX* Programming; Rochkind	013–011818–4	$32.95 cloth	_____
_____	8. System Software Tools; Biggerstaff	013–881772–3	$28.95 cloth	_____
_____	9. Crafting C Tools for the IBM PC; Campbell	013–188418–2	$21.95 paper	_____
_____	10. The UNIX* System User's Handbook; AT&T	013–937764–6	$16.95 paper	_____
_____	11. The Vi User's Handbook; AT&T	013–941733–8	$16.95 paper	_____
_____	12. The C Programmer's Handbook; AT&T	013–110073–4	$16.95 paper	_____
_____	13. AT&T Computer Software Catalog: MS DOS; AT&T	0–8359–9278–0	$19.95 paper	_____
_____	14. AT&T Computer Software Catalog: UNIX* System V; AT&T	0–8359–9279–0	$19.95 paper	_____
_____	15. The UNIX* C Shell Field Guide; Anderson/Anderson	013–937468–X	$23.95 paper	_____
_____	16. DOS/UNIX*: Becoming A Super User; Seyer/Mills	013–218645–4	$21.95 paper	_____
_____	17. UNIX* RefGuide; McNulty Development, Inc.	013–938952–0	$24.95 paper	_____
_____	18. Preparing Documents With UNIX*; Brown	013–699976–X	$21.95 cloth	_____
_____	19. Learning to Program in C; Plum	013–527854–6	$34.95 cloth	_____
_____	20. Programming in C With a Bit of UNIX*; Moore	013–730094–8	$22.95 paper	_____

Total $	_____
– discount (if appropriate)	_____
New Total $	_____

OVER PLEASE

AND TAKE ADVANTAGE OF THESE SPECIAL OFFERS!

a.) When ordering 3 or 4 copies (of the same or different titles), take 10% off the total list price (excluding sales tax, where applicable).

b.) When ordering 5 to 20 copies (of the same or different titles), take 15% off the total list price (excluding sales tax, where applicable).

c.) To receive a greater discount when ordering 20 or more copies, call or write:

Special Sales Department
College Marketing
Prentice-Hall
Englewood Cliffs, NJ 07632
201-592-2498

SAVE!
If payment accompanies order, plus your state's sales tax where applicable, Prentice-Hall pays postage and handling charges. Same return privilege refund guaranteed. Please do not mail in cash.

☐ **PAYMENT ENCLOSED**—shipping and handling to be paid by publisher (please include your state's tax where applicable).

☐ **SEND BOOKS ON 15-DAY TRIAL BASIS** & bill me (with small charge for shipping and handling).

Name_____

Address_____

City_____ State_____ Zip_____

I prefer to charge my ☐ Visa ☐ MasterCard

Card Number_____ Expiration Date_____

Signature_____
All prices listed are subject to change without notice.

Mail your order to: Prentice-Hall, Book Distribution Center, Route 59 at
Brook Hill Drive, West Nyack, NY 10994

Dept. 1   D–TMAR–LR(7)